W9-AFV-909

GREAT DANES
TODAY

DI JOHNSON

HOWELL
BOOK HOUSE

New York

Maxwell Macmillan Canada
Toronto

Maxwell Macmillan International
New York Oxford Singapore Sydney

Copyright © 1994 by Di Johnson.

All rights reserved. No part of this book may be reproduced or transmitted in any form or by any means, electronic or mechanical, including photocopying, recording, or by any information storage and retrieval system, without permission in writing from the Publisher.

Howell Book House
Macmillan Publishing Company
866 Third Avenue
New York, NY 10022

Maxwell Macmillan Canada, Inc.
1200 Eglinton Avenue East
Suite 200
Don Mills, Ontario M3C 3N1

Printed in Singapore

Macmillan Publishing Company is part of the Maxwell Communication Group of Companies.

Library of Congress Cataloging-in-Publication Data

Johnson, Di.
    Grerat Danes today / Di Johnson.
        p.   cm.
    ISBN 0-87605-186-7
    1. Great Danes. I. Title.
SF429.G7J62 1994
636.7'3–dc20   93-38102
                                                            CIP

Macmillan books are available at special discounts for bulk purchases for sales promotions, premiums, fund-raising, or educational use. For details, contact:

Special Sales Director
Macmillan Publishing Company
866 Third Avenue
New York, NY 10022

10 9 8 7 6 5 4 3 2 1

Contents

4

This book is dedicated to my friend, Audrey Sheppard, whose love for and understanding of this breed is so complete, surpassing any show ring victories or glories.

Acknowledgements

My thanks to all who helped and encouraged me to write this book.

To Audrey Sheppard, who so willing typed every word, without once criticising the text or complaining of my poor handwriting!

To her daughter, Alaine, whose artistic talent and knowledge of the breed helped with the line drawings.

To Bruce MacDonald, my old adversary, who so generously allowed me to use his research on hereditary conditions in Great Danes, once more proving his caring and responsible attitude to the breed.

To Jackie White (USA), Rosemary Hubrich (New Zealand) and to all those talented photographers and proud owners who provided photographs. I am sorry we could not use them all.

To my husband, Carl, whose confidence in my ability to do anything is both wonderful and terrifying.

To my longtime kennel manager and friend Stan Woolridge, whose loyalty is ever constant.

To the editor Julia Barnes, who invited me to write this book, supported me all the way, and didn't complain when I left her very little scope for editing!

Di Johnson

PREFACE

It is difficult for me to recall a time when I did not have a Great Dane around; it is impossible to envisage a time when I will not have a Great Dane around! From my teens into my fifties, I bred and exhibited Great Danes with a fervour and commitment that I remember with a breathless wonder. I was single-minded in my dedication to this magnificent breed.

I was fortunate that my husband, Carl, shared my enthusiasm. I was equally fortunate that he was a marvellous handler and could get absolutely the best from my Danes in the show ring. I was hopeless: I could make the best dog in the world look appalling and I *never* mastered 'running' – on my own, never mind with a Dane on a lead and in a straight line! Had it been left to me, not one of those Dicarl Great Danes would have carried the title of Champion. Many did! I was very proud of them; I still am. Now I no longer breed or exhibit, I can view the breed with an objectivity that was perhaps denied to me when my involvement was absolute.

Di Johnson pictured with one of the Dicarl Great Danes.

The Great Dane is a truly wonderful breed. It is said that once you have shared your life with a Great Dane you will always have another, and another, no other breed will do. They are called the 'Gentle Giants' and the 'Apollo of Dogs'. There is no compliment too great for this giant breed. A Dane will become your friend and understand you with a sensitivity surpassing any human understanding. Anyone who has felt the weight of a great heavy head on their shoulder or lap in times of sadness, will know exactly what I mean. Those who have been on the receiving end of that huge paw when attention was needed, or felt their arm taken by that strong but gentle mouth when your Dane wants to lead you somewhere, will be smiling in agreement now. These are Great Dane characteristics.

I have shared my life with this noble breed; today I only have four Danes; there were times when I had forty of them. I offer that depth of interest and those years of ownership as my credentials for writing a book on the most noble breed of all – the Great Dane.

INTRODUCTION

We just wanted a family pet. We decided on a Great Dane. A dog puppy, we thought; and set about locating a breeder. We contacted Olive Davies of the Oldmanor Great Danes, who told us that as first-time Dane owners, a bitch puppy would be much better and easier to cope with. This was not sales technique; she did not have a surfeit of puppy bitches; in fact, she did not have anything at all for sale at the time. She just 'sounded' as if she knew what she was talking about (we were later to find out just how accurate that impression was!), and so our search for a bitch pup ensued. Showing or breeding were not on our minds, but I did want a Great Dane that looked right – the way I thought a Dane should look. We saw several litters and nothing particularly appealed until I spotted a fourteen-week fawn watching me over a half-stable door at Nan Mudd's kennel. That was the one I wanted. She was not for sale, of course. Nan was running her on for showing and breeding. However, I have always subscribed to the theory that if you want something badly enough ... so Jayessem Jacamiranda became the Dane that every Dicarl can be traced back to.

We only showed Jacamiranda once or twice, mainly because she was so incredibly badly behaved, but the two first prizes we won at her first show sparked my interest in the breed. For the next couple of years, every weekend found us at a dog show, watching and learning.

THE FIRST LITTER
We had a litter with Jacamiranda. We went to Oldmanor: Olive Davies was the fountain of all knowledge to me, and whenever she gave me the chance I would be there, hanging on her every word. We bred two useful males: a fawn, Dicarl Domonic, who won well for us including a Reserve CC, and a brindle, Dicarl Demetrius, who went to Gwen and Alan Herbert and son, Leslie, who were later very successful with their Algynne Danes.

We bought a couple more Oldmanor bitches: one, Muffahiti, also won well including a Reserve CC – and we were hooked! The show bug had bitten Carl; he loved the handling, and I had made up my mind to be a breeder. This did not mean that I had decided to breed an occasional litter. Oh no! I had the gall to decide that I wanted to breed a line of Dicarl Great Danes that would be recognisable for their type and excellence just like the Oldmanors, Moonsfields, Blendons, Nightsgifts, Bringtonhills, Leesthorphills, Merrowleas, and all the other top kennels of that time.

MAKING PROGRESS

Jacamiranda had a litter by Ch. Meletaylon Of Oldmanor, who was out of the fabulous Ch. Meleta Of Oldmanor, and by a dog I so admired, Ch. Telaman Of Moonsfield. That produced a bitch called Dicarl Double-Up, and a wonderful promising dog pup called Double Top. Every breeder has their share of heartbreaks, and we were struck early by the blow of losing the dog puppy – a pup that even Dibbie Somerfield (another of my mentors) had described as "something special".

The bitch, Double-Up, was quite nice, but not a great show prospect. She was correct make and shape and had no glaring faults, but there was just not enough of her – not enough bone and not enough head. However, there was good breeding behind her, and I knew she could breed me something good. My thoughts were with her grandfather, Ch. Telaman, as by this time I had decided my strain would be based on the wonderful bodies of the Oldmanors and the glorious heads of the Moonsfields. I was very much a 'novice', remember!

Edna Harrild had bred a lovely brindle bitch called Ch. Telera Of Moonsfield, and mated her back to her grandfather, Telaman. A daughter of this mating was called Tartan Muse, owned by Aeron Clements of the Gowerfield Great Danes. Muse had the most beautiful head I have ever seen. She had a handsome brother called Texan, and another brother called Target. A huge strong brindle, Target was not a popular dog as he did lack a little quality. However, Double-Up had quality to spare. I think Target was only ever used three times at stud, and I talked the breeder into one of these matings! Playing a breeder's 'hunch', combined, of course, with knowledge of pedigrees, Target became the sire of Double-Up's famous daughters, Dicarl Tarbaby and Dicarl Tradub.

Edna Harrild came to see the litter of four puppies. She bought the two brindle dogs and they went abroad for show and breeding. In her own inimitable throwaway style, she nodded at the fawn bitch, Tarbaby, and said "That's a Champion"; turned her attention to the brindle, Tardub, and said "And that will breed you Champions."

Tarbaby had five litters, always producing quality Danes that bred on for me. Between litters she enjoyed success in the show ring, winning a CC, and several Reserve CCs. Breeding with, rather than showing, Tarbaby was doubly important, as Tardub sadly died after her first litter and she was the one I had such high hopes for in the whelping box. She was smashing, bigger and stronger than her sister – but she did give me a wonderful son before she died.

She was mated to a great dog, Ch. Gowerfield Galestorm Of Aysdaine, owned by Audrey Sheppard. 'Storm' excelled in breed type, and he was a son of Tartan Muse – the product of wonderful line breeding. Their son, Ch. Dicarl The Heavyweight, became one of the most influential stud dogs of his generation. He was exactly what I wanted. Just as he was everything I was looking for in a male, so similar remarks apply in bitch terms to Tarbaby's daughter, Ch. Dicarl The Lioness Of Jafrak, who was sired by Karina and Gordon Le Mare's Ch. Simba Of Helmlake.

Both The Lioness and The Heavyweight achieved great success in the show ring. Before they were even born, my plan had been to mate together the son and daughter of my 'Tar' litter sisters. They suited each other admirably. The Heavyweight was totally masculine with

Ch. Dicarl The Heavyweight ('The Heavy'): An ultra-masculine dog with great strength of head, typical expression, correct ears (size, shape and placement), and that wonderful, crested neck. Great temperament and a great sire. Perhaps, my all-time favourite great Dane male.

Diane Pearce.

Ch. Dicarl The Lioness Of Jafrak: A bitch of great size and substance, with great length of neck giving elegance and style. In her first litter to Heavyweight she threw three Champions.

Diane Pearce.

a wonderful head, great bone, with excellent front, sound in all departments and with great temperament and presence. Not the longest neck, but enough. The Lioness was a big girl with long elegant neck and regal bearing. Great temperament, a real showgirl. Just a touch straight behind, nothing serious, and I felt a litter would improve her in that area anyway. It did! My breeder's dream came true when an outstanding litter was born containing three puppies who went on to gain their titles, and others who proved their worth in the show ring and the whelping box.

The Heavyweight was siring Champions, and soon his son, Ch. The Weightlifter Of Dicarl would join him. The Lioness was whelping Champions, and soon her daughter, Ch. The Granddaughter would join her.

THE LINE DEVELOPS

My 'Tar' sisters did not have it all their own way – other bitches were being bred from and making their mark. Dicarl Muffahiti Of Oldmanor was a good bitch, typical of her breeding, and I chose to mate her to a very good dog, Ch. Walkmyll Kastor Of Clausentum, bred by Jean Lanning of Clausentum Great Danes and subsequently sold to Freda Lewis of Walkmyll Great Danes. Kastor was sired by Ch. Fergus Of Clausentum, a big impressive dog who was also the sire of Simba, The Lioness's sire. Line breeding devotees will understand my reasoning.

From Kaster to Muffahiti, I bred Dicarl Surprizing Stew and his sister Surprizing Sophie. Years later when Stew mated Tarbaby, the result was Ch. Dicarl The Pacemaker Of Meadvale. When Sophie was mated to The Heavyweight she produced two Champions, Ch. Dicarl The Hot News and Ch. Dicarl The Hotentot. Line breeding was working!

Muffahiti was mated again, this time to Keith and Maureen Taylor's Treslyan Tudor Minstrel, a brindle who was unlucky not to gain his title. He was a powerful, handsome, typy male, not as 'overdone' as his sire. Who was his sire? Target Of Moonsfield, father of my 'Tar' sisters! Minstrel's dam was a very lovely Oldmanor-type bitch with a lovely body shape, and oozing quality. (This was the mating I had urged those years before to the less-than-in-demand Target.) Ch. Dicarl The Prizefighter came from the Muffahiti/Minstrel alliance. He was a huge brindle dog with a great neck and headpiece. In terms of construction, he was not the best dog I ever bred. Possibly because of this, I underestimated his value as a stud dog, using him only sparingly. Time showed his value as a grandsire and he features in many Champions' pedigrees. He was born within three weeks of The Weightlifter, and that fawn boy was such a star he overshadowed others of his generation. Justly, the first Champion he sired was Ch. Aysdaine Lion, cleverly line-bred by Audrey Sheppard, using a Storm daughter to a Storm grandson.

THE DICARL TYPE

The line was established: recognisable type was being produced in every litter. We enjoyed success in the show ring, but my preoccupation was always with the Dicarl line. When good, typical, sound bitches came to our dogs, I would study their pedigrees and if I felt they were suitable, complementary to the line, I would buy in a puppy, thereby bringing in slightly new blood.

Ch. The Granddaughter Of Dicarl: Litter sister to The Weightlifter. She was a controversial bitch as she was very large, with great strength and substance – exactly my idea of a brood bitch. Her offspring went on to be multiple CC winners. She was mated to sons of her brother, i.e. her nephews, as part of the line-breeding programme. Diane Pearce.

Ch. The Wrestler Of Dicarl: A Weightlifter son – a quality male with excellent movement. A sire of Champions, including The Alliance and The Rolling Stone, and of many bitches who went on to produce Champions.

Thomas Fall.

My line breeding was close: half brother to sister matings worked well – Heavyweight daughters to Weightlifter sons and vice versa. In time, two Weightlifter sons joined the stud team. The first was Ch. Dicarl The Contender of Dicarl, who was out of a lovely Endroma bitch, bred by Peter and Rae Russell out of their very lovely Champion bitch, who had beautiful movement. Being predominantly Oldmanor bred, line breeding was maintained. Shirley and Charlie Verity mated the most typical Gaymiles bitch to Weightlifter, and after visiting the litter, I brought home another fawn male, who became Ch. The Wrestler of Dicarl, a dog who sired particularly good bitches for me.

Ch. The Granddaughter was mated to both of her brother's sons in turn. To The Contender she produced Ch. Dicarl Tendellie, and to The Wrestler she produced a son, Ch. Dicarl The Alliance With Algynne, who went to my long-time favourite owners, the Herberts, who had given Dicarl Demetrius such a happy life, years before. The Kralls had kept the litter sister to The Granddaughter, and they line-bred her to The Wrestler, which gave them Ch. Jafrak Jinger Cookie. They also bred a bitch called Baby Grand Of Dicarl,who, when mated to The Contender, gave young Les Herbert Ch. Dicarl The Liaison With Algynne. I continued to line-breed and continued to breed Champions. More important than titles, I continued to breed Great Danes that I honestly believed to be true to type and to the breed Standard. This is the story of how one kennel established a line, and I will admit I was lucky!

Chapter One

ORIGINS OF THE GREAT DANE

THE BREED IN ANTIQUITY

The Great Dane is a dog of such majesty, such awe-inspiring nobility, such aristocratic bearing that one imagines it to be a breed of ancient lineage and great antiquity. The overall balance, ratio and conformation of the breed is essentially 'dog shaped'. A child given a pencil and asked to draw 'a dog' would probably produce the basic structure and shape of the Great Dane.

Certainly dogs of Dane-like appearance were found depicted on the walls of the temples and palaces of the Assyrian Kings. Two pictures of old Assyrian monuments are preserved to this day: one, a relief plate came from a Babylonian temple built 2,000 years BC, showing an Assyrian man with a powerful Dane-like dog on a leash, while the second picture shows dogs pursuing two horses who have been hit by arrows. These dogs appear powerful specimens of boarhound type, not dissimilar to Great Danes as we know them.

Another suggestion of the breed's antiquity is a Grecian coin in the Royal Museum in Munich, which dates from the 5th century BC, showing a dog resembling the Great Dane. There is also a wall relief from an Assyrian castle, built about 900 B.C. On this, the dog depicted has a more elegant build and would suggest a swifter hunting dog, but again can be seen as Dane-like.

History shows that the Persians, Greeks and Romans kept Dane- and Mastiff-like dogs. It is likely that the more cultured Romans were interested in breeding pure-bred dogs of two types both of which could be described as resembling a Dane. However, one was heavier and more powerful, bred for fighting; the other was of a more elegant build for hunting purposes. It is known that the Romans imported British dogs of Molossian ancestry which the Phoenicans had taken into Britain in the 6th century. These dogs were said to be able to break the neck of an ox! So we can believe, if we choose, that Dane-like dogs have existed in many parts of the world for a great many centuries.

THE MIDDLE AGES

Enormous packs of boars roamed the mid-European forests, and it was a favourite pastime of the gentry of the day to hunt them. Essential in this sporting pursuit were dogs, known as Boar-hounds, who were certainly the ancestors of the Great Dane. Illustrations of 14th and

Ch. Markrich Michelle: The Great Dane is a dog of great nobility.   *Lenny Ludham.*

Ch. Devarro Mr Sullivan: The Great Dane was bred to hunt wild boar, and dogs should retain the substance and muscular power, so that they look as though they are still capable of working.

Roger Chambers.

15th century hunting scenes show dogs known as Alaunts. Writings describe them as gigantic, measuring as much as 30-32 inches at the withers.

Many of the boar-hunting dogs in England had been bred by the cross of Mastiff and Irish Greyhounds, some of which were taken to France and Spain and bred with the European Boarhounds. In the North of England at Lyme Park, during the 16th and 17th centuries, a type of dog resembling a Great Dane, known as the Lyme Mastiff, was bred and highly prized in both England and the rest of Europe. A visit to Lyme Hall, now a National Trust property, would be of interest to those breed fanciers with enquiring minds. It seems likely that these handsome dogs played a part in the development of our breed.

Dr Morrell Mackenzie's book, *Great Danes Past and Present*, published early in this century and acknowledged as *the* book of the breed, suggests that the Great Dane has existed continuously in Great Britain from the earliest times, with confusion between the Irish Wolfhound and the Great Dane, the two breeds existing side by side but also cross-mated indiscriminately. Mrs Lee Booker, in her book *Great Danes of Today*, writes: "The history of the breed, if it is to be written at all would fill the *Encyclopaedia Britannica.*" Speculation runs riot; romantic, wishful thinking provides colour; and who will deny that

Ulla Magnusson's Airways Danes. A fully mature brindle showing great dignity, and a fawn puppy showing the most typical expression. Boar hounds' ears were cropped to prevent injury. This practice was banned in Britain in the 19th Century, but Great Danes still have their ears cropped in America and many parts of Europe.

David Dalton.

such a majestic breed should have always existed and found favour?

BOARHOUND ANCESTRY

Credence must be given to the Boarhound ancestry of our breed – indeed traits and instincts persist to this day. From paintings, illustrations, and writings, we know that the dogs were used to chase the boar, effect a purchase on the formidable animal's ears and pull him to the ground. In play and excitement, the Dane of today will often grab an arm or sleeve in similar style. Some reaction is often shown when our Danes are in close proximity with pigs and goats.

I hesitate to tell this sad story, but years ago we decided that as goat's milk was so good for the dogs, we would purchase a couple of goats of our own. They had their own large paddock and the exercise was proving quite successful, if tiring, with twice-daily milking – until one day, two of our Dane bitches, good-natured, mild-mannered ladies, decided on closer investigation of the unfamiliar four-legged animals in the far paddock. The goats took fear and began to run; the Danes were thrilled and pursued with enthusiasm. Natural instincts came to the fore and those poor goats were effectively 'boar hunted' and pulled to the ground by their ears. The Danes were very excited, with faraway looks in their eyes, and took a deal of calming ...

Because the Boarhound heritage theory is generally accepted, there are those who believe the Great Dane belongs in the Hound Group rather than the Working Group. Whatever the Group, it is important that we remember a breed's original function, as breed type is, in part, created by the dog still having the ability to do the job for which it was originally intended – or at least, looking as if it could! A Great Dane that is gross, with clumsy heavy body on short stumpy legs, would never have the speed and grace to catch a wild boar, and if it did, those great bulbous-pointed pigeon forechests we see now, would prohibit the animal actually getting close enough to the boar to grab its ear! The over-tall, fine-boned, swan-necked Dane would fare no better; without the substance and muscular power, these willowy Danes would not survive a confrontation with any wild boar.

Boar hounds needed to be strong, powerful and agile. Many sustained horrendous injuries and, of course, ears were one of the most vulnerable parts of the body. For this reason, they were cropped. However, in Britain the practice came to an end when the Prince of Wales, later to become King Edward VII, expressed disapproval. In 1895 a rule was passed by The Kennel Club forbidding the cropping of Great Danes. After the turn of the century it was prohibited to show a Dane with cropped ears. A law was never passed; it is not an illegal practice, but the governing body, the Kennel Club, passed a rule and it was, and is, adhered to. The step caused a great decline in the popularity of the breed in Britain. Cropped Danes were still being imported from Germany, but the quarantine conditions imposed at that time, due to a rabies scare, contributed to uncertain times in the breed in England.

WHAT'S IN A NAME?

Why is our breed called the Great Dane? Why not the Great English or the Great German? It is unlikely that any credit for the breed actually goes to Denmark. Even in England, the dogs were known as both the German Mastiff and the English Dogge. The breed was also known as Ulmer Doggen, Danish Doggen, and Deustche Dogge; in France it was known as the Grand Danois. Germany claims the breed as its own: the national dog of the Fatherland – the Deutsche Dogge. There is some dispute over this, but the claim cannot be disproved. Certainly, great credit must go to the German breeders of that time for breeding Great Danes that formed the basis of the breed as we know it today.

Chapter Two

OWNING A GREAT DANE

A Great Dane is a dog to be proud of, a dog that commands attention and invites admiration from all who see members of the breed. Pride of ownership manifests itself on a daily basis for those who own a Great Dane. Just walking down the road with a Dane on a lead will create interest from passers-by, who are, understandably, impressed by the great size, the regal demeanour, and the instant appeal that this breed possesses.

The Great Dane's appeal is undeniable. I am always pleased and surprised – although I should be used to it by now – by the vast number of people from all walks of life who speak about Great Danes with something almost bordering on reverence! There is a sort of awe and envy in their faces and in their voices when they learn that you own a Great Dane. They all have a story to tell of a Dane they used to know, often in childhood, often owned by a relation, always remembered with great fondness and respect. Even people 'in' dogs with long-standing and successful kennels of, presumably, an equally appealing breed, will generously concede that a Great Dane is something special: a breed they greatly admire, a breed they have always wanted to own.

WHY A GREAT DANE?
This is a reasonable question, usually asked by a proud and protective breeder who, while the prospective purchaser is deciding whether or not to buy the puppy, is deciding whether or not to let them *have* the puppy. Will they be responsible owners? Will they love and care for the puppy? Are they prepared to change their lifestyle to suit the new arrival; change their sports car for an estate model?

During the viewing and interviewing that is taking place on both sides, the breeder will often ask: "What makes you want a Great Dane?" The answer is nearly always the same: "Oh, I have always wanted a Great Dane." It is said with such feeling, and gives assurance to an anxious breeder that this is no 'impulse buy'; here is a person fulfilling a lifelong dream to own a Great Dane.

ONCE A DANE, ALWAYS A DANE
Long established breeders will tell you of the great proportion of puppy customers who come back for another – and another. It is a fact that once you have owned a Dane you

Once you have owned a Great Dane – you will always want to own the breed.

always will – or you will always want to own this breed, although sometimes circumstances will not allow. The vast majority of my puppies over the years were replacements for much-loved Danes bought from me eight, nine or ten years previously. These are, of course, the best homes of all. The owners understand the breed and their requirements, and they want another just like 'Sally' or 'Bruno', with the same temperament and the same loving ways.

Be warned – if you are teetering on the brink of having your first Great Dane, it is better than even money that it will not be your last!

LIFE WITH A DANE
Well, it will never be lonely, it is unlikely to be uneventful, it certainly will not be boring! The Dane will become a part of your life, a very important part – a Dane is not prepared to be overlooked. This has very little to do with size, in fact your Dane will take up remarkably little room. It is quite astounding how small a Dane can be when the desire to occupy a certain space is paramount. To watch a fully grown Dane insinuate themselves into an armchair, brings meaning to the 'quart in a pint pot' expression. You think the dog cannot

possibly be comfortable curled up and squashed like that. However, the Dane will heave the most enormous sigh to indicate great ecstasy, and will settle in absolute contentment. When you understand the reason why a Dane is prepared to fit into any space available, and with relish, you will understand the breed !

A Great Dane just wants to be with 'their' people, 'their' person, 'their' family. They will put up with any inconvenience as long as they can be with you, included in all you do, at all times.

THE FAMILY DOG

I cannot stress too strongly the Great Dane's desire to be a part of the family. A Dane, perhaps more than any other breed, needs people, their own people, their family. The breed does not take easily to strangers: they have an immense loyalty to their own family, but can be a little stand-offish with outsiders. They have a natural dignity and can be quite appalled

A Great Dane is a great family dog and will be loyal to children and adults alike.

by over-familiarity from total strangers. Their 'touch me not' attitude with new people can be overcome if the people are encouraged to wait for the Dane to initiate the friendship. If they will actually ignore the Dane, the Dane's natural curiosity will get the better of them and they will soon investigate and allow the usual admiration and affection to take place. Nevertheless, people outside of the Dane's immediate family circle are really quite superfluous to our breed. A Dane is, in the true sense of the words, a 'family dog'.

While I would never encourage anyone to obtain a Great Dane as a guard dog – the very size and depth of bark will act as a deterrent. Only the bravest or most foolhardy intruder would continue when confronted with a Great Dane in full voice. A Dane at full height and voicing disapproval is a truly awesome sight. The wish to protect the family is perfectly natural to the breed, and responsible owners will encourage or modify the trait to sensible proportions.

NO BAD DOGS – ONLY BAD OWNERS

Temperament is an inherited quality. A wise puppy purchaser will buy from a kennel or a line noted for its good temperament. A wise breeder will wish to discuss temperament with a new owner. If the first question from prospective puppy purchasers was: "How much are your puppies?" followed by "How tall will the puppy grow?" I would rapidly lose interest in selling them one of my precious pups.

If they asked: "Do the mother and father have good temperaments?" they would be invited to meet the sire and dam, grandparents, aunts and uncles, and while they were assessing the temperaments of the dogs in my kennels, I would be assessing theirs! If there were children in the family, I would insist they came along. If the children were out of control, climbing over the furniture, opening drawers, knocking things over and generally behaving like little ruffians, then I would consider that family unsuitable for one of my pups. For as surely as temperament is an inherited quality, it can be moulded, developed and even changed to a detrimental degree, by environment.

Good dogs come not only from good bloodlines but also from good owners. Danes, being so dependent on family closeness, tend to emulate the personalities of their owners. A boisterous family will be likely to have a boisterous Dane; a timid, jumpy person will probably have a Dane showing similar traits. Just as surely, providing they bought sensibly, a happy, well-balanced, sensible family will enjoy life with a Great Dane displaying the typical temperament of the breed.

I defend the heading of this section, 'No bad dogs – only bad owners', by telling you that after a lifetime in dogs, I have met very few dogs I could not like and even love, given time. I certainly could not say that about people – could you?

ARRIVING HOME

Your new puppy has left the warmth and security of mother and littermates and is now alone for the first time. Most Dane pups take this in their stride; they are interested in new surroundings and thrilled to be the 'only one' getting all the attention. However, some pups may be more sensitive or thoughtful, and they may feel a little lost out in the great big world. They may miss the competition of littermates around the food bowl. They may feel

A puppy has a lot to get used when first arriving home, and will need to be introduced to all members of its new family. A Dane thrives on human companionship, but will also enjoy the company of a canine companion.

over-awed by the unusual activities of the new owner's lifestyle. These reactions are unlikely, but possible; all will be overcome very quickly with your reassurance.

FEEDING YOUR DANE

It is often imagined that such a large dog will need vast amounts of food, and that the cost of feeding a Great Dane could be prohibitive. Not so. Danes are not generally greedy dogs; they certainly will not eat you out of house and home. It is true that a Dane puppy with tremendous growth-rate needs to be fed extremely well (reputable breeders will provide a detailed diet sheet), and rearing a Dane puppy has no room for penny-pinching. It is often said by senior Dane breeders that what you put into a puppy is what you get out in terms of the mature specimen!

I agree wholeheartedly with the theory that a Dane puppy needs the very best of rearing. A puppy is born with the potential to make a certain size – not just height, but also bone and substance. Given the correct rearing, the pup will realise full potential. Inadequately reared, the young adult can lack bone and width, and the great size and substance that makes this breed so commanding.

However, once your Dane is fully grown, a correct maintenance diet, to keep the dog in the peak of health and fitness, is well within the confines of a normal family budget. There are so many excellent, balanced foods available these days, with protein levels and feeding ratios developed by experts on nutrition, that it ill behoves me (an amateur) to comment. It is important to follow the diet recommended by the breeder when your puppy first arrives home. If you try tempting the puppy to eat with different foods, this will result in an upset tummy and a possible fussy feeder for the future. Anxiety about the pup's appetite is a regular occurrence among new Dane owners. A bright-minded puppy will sense your anxiety and 'play you up' over feeding, if you allow.

I admit that I made every mistake in the book with my first Dane. I was so anxious for her to grow up big and strong, I pandered to her every whim. If she turned her nose up at dog food, I offered her a selection of whatever might take her fancy. The day I caught myself

Great Dane puppies need the very best of rearing. They need to develop in bone and substance – not just in height.

with a pan of freshly cooked sausages in one hand and a packet of sliced beef in gravy in the other, pleading with her to choose one of them, I realised she had the upper hand! She lived to ten years of age, and all through her life would sniff disdainfully at her lovingly prepared food bowl and then look up at me as if to say "Don't fancy that – what else have you got?"

So, put the puppy's recommended food down at the recommended time. If it is not eaten within twenty minutes, do not show concern, just pick it up and repeat the process in due course. One of the advantages of buying a puppy from a reputable breeder is that they give 'after sales' service. They are only a telephone-call away and will give good advice and reassurance.

GETTING USED TO THE CAR
Most Dane pups take to travelling in the car as a duck takes to water. They may take an interest in the passing scene, bracing themselves on chunky, front legs when the brake is applied – some of mine even looked right and left at crossroads – or they may fall fast asleep, resting peacefully through the most traumatic of journeys.

Your Dane will certainly enjoy the luxuries of life and will be only too happy to relax on the sofa!

Occasionally a pup may be susceptible to car travel sickness. Most pups will outgrow this problem, just as children do. However, the unhappy pup, drooling saliva and possibly vomiting, can be helped by animal travel sickness pills, given at least two hours before the journey. Ask your vet for advice.

It is wise to allow the puppy to get used to the car from the very beginning. The pup can start off by sitting in the car while it is stationary in the drive for short periods of time. The next step is very short journeys to open areas where the pup can be released for exercise and play. This means the puppy will look forward to car travel from an early age, and car problems never arise.

EXERCISING YOUR DANE

Your Dane loves you and wants to please you. I write this with total confidence: I have never yet met a Dane who failed in this quality. So if you want to walk for miles daily, your Dane will willingly, happily accompany you. Exercise is very important because it is part of your Dane's time with you: something you share – having fun together.

Does your Dane actually *need* hours of exercise daily? No, not really. A Dane probably requires as much exercise as the average dog. A good gallop to stretch their legs daily would be ideal. Two or three joyous, enthusiastic circuits of a field, running full-tilt, ears flying, will bring your Dane back to you, panting and looking for praise, and with a readable

'The Apollo of Dogs: The Dane is loyal and trustworthy, dignified and aristocratic.

expression that says: "Didn't I do well? Let's go home now, have a drink and relax on the settee in front of the fire."

Good feeding and correct exercise will enhance your dog's health and appearance, build up muscle tone, and make your dog feel good. Individual dogs have individual requirements. If you have the correct relationship with your Dane, you will appreciate your Dane's requirements. You will recognise those times when your Dane is 'full of it', raring to go, needing to let off steam, wanting to go for a walk. You will be equally understanding of those times when your Dane snuggles closer to the fire, lazily content, enjoying the comforts of home life.

THE APOLLO OF DOGS
The breed has earned this honorary title; they are also known as 'Gentle Giants'. They are loyal and dependable, trusting and trustworthy, dignified and aristocratic, loving and playful. They are never spiteful and never, ever, treacherous. I admit I am biased; but then, anyone else who has had any contact with the breed will, I am sure, tell you similar things. They are a wonderful breed.

Chapter Three

THE BREED STANDARD

The breed Standard is the blueprint for the breed – a template, an attempt to describe in words the concept and proportions of what is considered to be the ideal specimen of the breed in question. The Breed Standard should be treated with respect and referred to with regularity. It must be the breeder's and the judge's bible.

I only wish it could be handed down from some great Mount, on Tablets of Stone; perhaps then its importance would be taken more seriously. Without responsible adherence to the Breed Standard by breeders and judges alike, the breed will drift away from its original form and function; true breed type will be lost – the breed will change.

The argument used by those reluctant to embrace the breed Standard (probably because the Dane they are showing currently does not fit it) is that it is only words, and therefore open to interpretation. I have even heard it said that as long as a Dane has four legs, a head and a tail, it can be seen to fit the Standard! Perhaps the most irritating remark quite frequently heard is "Well, I know what *my* idea of a Great Dane is; I know what I like."

Those who choose to disregard, misinterpret or make light of the Breed Standard are doing the breed a great disservice. The breed has stood the test of time, it was here long before any of us came along. During our involvement with the breed, our duty should be to preserve, to nurture, to maintain the breed at a level of excellence. We should see ourselves, I suggest, as caretakers of the breed. Our commitment during our short time with Great Danes – when seen in relation to the breed's existence – is to *take care* of them, not to change them out of all recognition.

The Great Dane's country of origin is Germany, and therefore I have reproduced the German breed Standard, followed by the British and American Standards.

GERMAN BREED STANDARD

GENERAL APPEARANCE AND CHARACTER: The Great Dane combines pride, strength and elegance in its noble appearance and big, strong, well-coupled body. It is the Apollo of all the breeds of dogs. The Dane strikes one by its very expressive head; it does not show any nervousness even in the greatest excitement and has the appearance of a noble statue. In temperament it is friendly, loving and affectionate with its

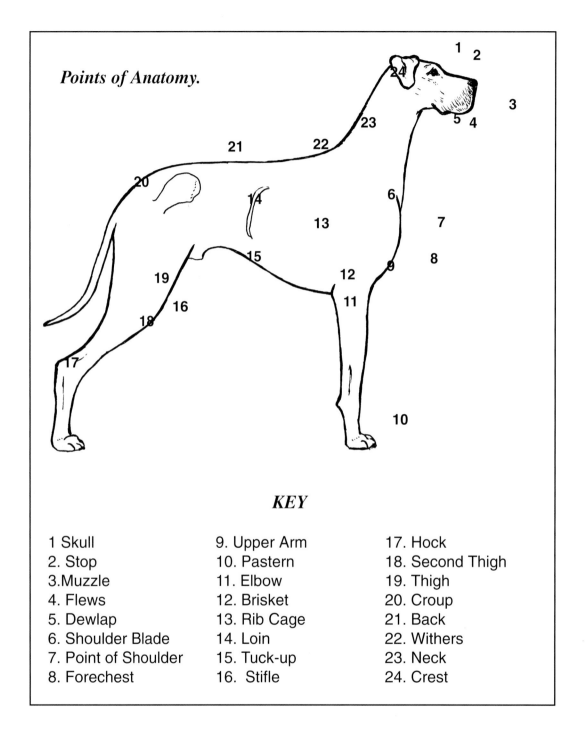

Points of Anatomy.

KEY

1 Skull	9. Upper Arm	17. Hock
2. Stop	10. Pastern	18. Second Thigh
3.Muzzle	11. Elbow	19. Thigh
4. Flews	12. Brisket	20. Croup
5. Dewlap	13. Rib Cage	21. Back
6. Shoulder Blade	14. Loin	22. Withers
7. Point of Shoulder	15. Tuck-up	23. Neck
8. Forechest	16. Stifle	24. Crest

masters, especially with children, but retiring and mistrustful with strangers. In time of danger the dog is courageous and not afraid of attacks, caring only for the defence of its master and the latter's property.

HEAD: Elongated, narrow, striking, full of expression, finely chiselled (especially the part under the eyes), with strongly accentuated stop. Seen from the side, the brow should be sharply broken off from the bridge of the nose. The forehead and bridge of the nose must run into each other in a straight and parallel line. Seen from the front, the head must appear narrow, the bridge of the nose must be as broad as possible; the cheek muscles should be only slightly accentuated, but in no case must they be prominent.

The muzzle must be full of lip, as much as possible vertically blunted in front, and show well-accentuated lip-angle. The underjaw should be neither protruding nor retrograding. The same length as the back of the head, from the stop to the slightly accentuated occiput. Seen from all sides, the head should appear angular and settled in its outer lines, but at the same time it should harmonize entirely with the general appearance of the Great Dane in every way.
Faults: Falling-off line of brow; an elevated, falling-off or compressed bridge of nose; too little or no stop; too narrow a bridge of nose; the back of the head wedge-shaped; too round a skull (apple head); cheeks too pronounced; snipy muzzle. Also loose lips hanging over the underjaw, which can be deceptive as to a full, deep muzzle. It is preferable for the head to be short and striking, rather than long, shallow and expressionless.

EYES (in general): Of medium size, round, as dark as possible, with gay, hearty expression, the eyebrows well developed.
Faults: Eyes light, cutting, amber-yellow, light blue or water blue, or of two different colours; too low-hanging eyelids with prominent tear glands or very red conjunctiva tunica.

EARS: Set on high, not too far apart, of good length, cropped to a point.
Faults: Ears set too low, laterally, cropped too short or not uniformly; standing too much over or even lying on the head; not carried erect or semi-drooping ears (uncropped Danes should not win).

NOSE: Large, black, running in a straight line with the bridge.
Faults: Nose light-coloured, with spots or cleft.

TEETH: Large and strong, white, fitting into each other, which is correct when the lower incisors fit tightly into the upper ones just as two scissor blades.
Faults: The incisors of the lower jaw are protruding (undershot) or those of the upper jaw protrude (overshot). Also, when the incisors of both jaws stand one upon another ('crackers'), for in this case the teeth wear out prematurely. Imperceptible deviations

are allowed. Distemper teeth should be objected to as they hide caries; likewise when the teeth look broken or are brown. Tartar is also undesirable.

NECK: Long, dry, muscular and sinewy, without strongly developed skin or dewlap, it should taper slightly from the chest to the head, be nicely ascending, and set on high with a well-formed nape.
Faults: Neck short, thick with loose skin or dewlap.

SHOULDERS: The shoulder-blade should be long and slanting; it should join the bone of the upper arm in the same position in the shoulder joint, as far as possible forming a right angle, in order to allow roomy movement. The withers should be well accentuated.
Faults: Straight or loose shoulders; the former occur when the shoulder-blade is not sufficiently slanting, the latter when the elbows turn outwards.

CHEST: As large as possible, the ribs well-rounded, deep in front, reaching up to the elbow joints.
Faults: Chest narrow, shallow with flat ribs; chest bone protruding too much.

BODY: The back straight, short and tight, the body should be as far as possible square in relation to the height; a somewhat longer back is allowed in bitches. The loins should be lightly arched and strong, the croup running fully imperceptibly into the root of the tail. The belly should be well tucked up backwards, and forming a nicely arched line with the inside of the chest.
Faults: Saddle-back, roach-back, or when the height of the hindquarters exceeds that of the forequarters (overbuilt); too long a back, since the gait then suffers (rolling gait); the croup falling off at a slant; belly hanging down and badly showing teats in bitches.

TAIL: Of medium length, only reaching to the hocks, set on high and broad, but tapering to a point; hanging down straight at rest, slightly curved (sword-like) in excitement or running, not carried over the back.
Faults: Tail too long, too low set on, carried too high over the back, or curled over the back; turned sideways; broken off or docked (it is forbidden to shorten the tail to obtain the prescribed length); brush tail (when the hair on the inside is too long) is undesirable. It is forbidden to shave the tail.

FRONT LEGS: The continuation of the elbows of the forearm must now reach the round of the chest, but must be well let down, must not appear either inwards or outwards, but should lie in equal flatness with the shoulder joint. The upper front or side – absolutely straight down to the pasterns.
Faults: Elbows turning in or out; if turning in, their position impedes movement by rubbing against the ribs and at the same time turns the whole lower part of the legs and causes the feet to turn outwards; if turning out, the reverse happens and the toes

are forced inwards. Both these positions are a fault, but the latter does not hinder movement since it does not cause any rubbing of the elbows against the chest wall. If the forelegs stand too wide apart the feet are forced to turn inwards while in the case of the 'narrow' stand brought about by the narrow chest, the front legs incline towards each other and the toes again turn outwards. The curving of the joint of the root of the front foot is equally faulty; it points to weakness of the pasterns (soft pastern) or in foot-roots (tarsus), and often causes flat feet and splayed toes. Swelling over the joint of the tarsus points mainly to diseases of the bone (rickets).

HIND LEGS: The buttocks of the hind legs should be broad and muscular, the under-thighs long, strong and forming a not too obtuse angle with the short tarsus. Seen from behind, the hocks should appear absolutely straight, sloping neither outwards nor inwards.
Faults: If the knee joint is turned too far outwards, the under-thigh forces the hock inwards and the dog is then 'cow-hocked', not a nice position at all. Too broad a stand in the hocks is just as ugly, as it impedes the light movement. In profile, the well developed hind thigh is too short and the dog is forced to keep it vertically to the straight tarsus. If the bone of the hind thighs is too long (in relation to the forelimbs), then the hind thighs are diagonally bent together, and this is not at all good.

FEET: Roundish, turned neither inwards nor outwards. The toes should be short, highly arched and well closed, the nails short, strong and black.
Faults: Splayed toes, hare-feet, toes turned inwards or outwards; further, the fifth toes on the hind legs placed higher (dewclaw); also if the nails are too long, or light in colour.

MOVEMENT: Fleeting, stepping out.
Faults: Short strides which are not free; narrow or rolling gait; ambling gait.

COAT: Very short and thick, lying close and shiny.
Faults: Hair too long, lopped hair (due to bad feeding, worms and faulty care).

COLOUR
(a) Brindle Danes: Ground colour from light golden fawn to dark golden fawn, always with well-defined black stripes. The more intense the ground colour and the stronger the stripes, the more striking is the effect. Small white patches on the chest and toes, or light eyes and nails, are not desirable.
Faults: Silver-blue or biscuit-coloured ground colour, washed out stripes, white streak between the eyes up to the nose, white ring on the neck, white 'socks' and white tip of tail. Danes with such markings should be excluded from winning prizes.
(b) Fawn Danes: Colour, fawn-golden and fawn to dark golden fawn; black mask as well as black nails are desired. The golden-fawn colour should always be preferred.
Faults: Silver grey, blue grey, biscuit fawn and dirty fawn colour should be placed

lower in the award list. For white markings see (a) above.

(c) Blue Danes: The colour should be as far as possible steel blue, without any tinge of fawn or black. Lighter eyes are allowed in blue Danes.

Faults: Fawn-blue or black-blue colour, too light or wall eyes. Regarding the white markings see (a) above.

(d) Black Danes: Should be wallflower black, shiny with dark eyes and black nails.

Faults: Yellow-brown or blue-black colour; light or amber coloured eyes; lightly coloured nails. Danes with too many white markings should be lower in the list of awards. Under white markings it should be noted that a white streak on the throat, spots on the chest, on toes (only up to the pasterns) are allowed, but Danes with a white blaze, white ring on neck, white 'socks' or white belly, should be debarred from winning.

(e) Harlequins: The ground colour should always be white, without any spots, with patches running all over the body, well-torn, irregular, wallflower black (a few small grey or brownish patches are admitted but not desired). Nose and nails should be black, but a nose with black spots or a fleshy nose are allowed. Eyes should be dark; light or two-coloured eyes are permitted but not desired.

Faults: White ground colour with several large black patches; bluish-grey ground colour; water-light, red or bleary eyes.

The following Danes should be excluded from winning :-

1. White Danes without any black markings; albinos, as well as deaf Danes.

2. 'Mantle' Harlequins, i.e. Danes having a large patch – like a mantle running all over the body, and only the legs, neck and tip of the tail are white.

3. So-called 'Porcelain' Harlequins, i.e. Danes with mostly blue-grey, fawn or even brindle patches.

SIZE: The height at the shoulder should not be under 76cm (30 ins or 2.5ft) but preferably should measure about 80cm; in bitches, not under 70cm, but preferably 75cm and over.

Reproduced by kind permission of the Deutsche Doggen Club.

BRITISH BREED STANDARD

GENERAL APPEARANCE: Very muscular, strongly though elegantly built with a look of dash and daring, of being ready to go anywhere and do anything. Head and neck carried high, tail in line with back, or slightly upwards, but never curled over hindquarters. Elegance of outline and grace of form most essential.

CHARACTERISTICS: Alert expression, powerful, majestic action displaying dignity.

TEMPERAMENT: Kindly without nervousness, friendly and outgoing.

HEAD AND SKULL: Head, taken altogether, gives idea of great length and strength of jaw. Muzzle or foreface broad, skull proportionately narrow so that the whole head when viewed from above and in front, has appearance of equal breadth throughout. Length of head in proportion to height of dog. Length from nose to point between the eyes about equal or preferably of greater length than from this point to back of occiput. Skull flat, slight indentation running up centre, occiputal peak not prominent. Decided rise or brow over the eyes but not abrupt stop between them; face well chiselled, well filled in below eyes with no appearance of being pinched; foreface long, of equal depth throughout. Cheeks showing as little lumpiness as possible, compatible with strength. Underline of head, viewed in profile, runs almost in a straight line from corner of lip to corner of jawbone, allowing for fold of lip, but with no loose skin hanging down.

Bridge of nose very wide, with slight ridge where cartilage joins bone. (This is a characteristic of breed.) Nostrils large, wide and open, giving blunt look to nose. Lips hang squarely in front, forming right-angle with upper line of foreface.

EYES: Fairly deep set, not giving the appearance of being round, of medium size and preferably dark. Wall or odd eyes permissible in harlequins.

EARS: Triangular, medium size, set high on skull and folded forward, not pendulous.

MOUTH: Teeth level. Jaws strong with a perfect, regular and complete scissor bite, i.e. the upper teeth closely overlapping the lower teeth and set square to the jaws.

NECK: Neck long, well-arched, quite clean and free from loose skin, held well up, well set in shoulders, junction of head and neck well-defined.

FOREQUARTERS: Shoulders muscular, not loaded, well sloped back, with elbows well under body. Forelegs perfectly straight with big flat bone.

BODY: Very deep, brisket reaching elbow, ribs well sprung, belly well drawn up. Back and loins strong, latter slightly arched.

HINDQUARTERS: Extremely muscular, giving strength and galloping power. Second thigh long and well developed, good turn of stifle, hocks set low, turning neither in nor out.

FEET: Cat-like, turning neither in nor out. Toes well arched and close, nails strong and curved. Nails preferably dark in all coat colours, except harlequins, where light are permissible.

GAIT/MOVEMENT: Action lithe, springy and free, covering ground well. Hocks move freely with driving action, head carried high.

TAIL: Thick at the root, tapering towards end, reaching to or just below hocks.

Carried in a straight line level with back, when dog is moving, slightly curved towards end, but never curling or carried over back.

COAT: Short, dense and sleek looking, never inclined to roughness.

COLOUR

Brindles: must be striped, ground colour from lightest buff to deepest orange, stripes always black, eyes and nails preferably dark, dark shadings on head and ears acceptable.

Fawns: colour varies from lightest buff to deepest orange, dark shadings on head and ears acceptable, eyes and nails preferably dark.

Blues: colour varies from light grey to deep slate, the nose and eyes may be blue.

Blacks: black is black.

In all above colours white is only permissible on chest and feet, but is not desirable even there. Nose always black except in blues and harlequins. Eyes and nails preferably dark.

Harlequins: pure white underground with preferably all black patches or all blue patches, having appearance of being torn. Light nails permissible. In harlequins, wall eyes, pink noses, or butterfly noses permissible but not desirable.

SIZE: Minimum height of an adult dog over eighteen months 76 cms (30ins); bitches 71 cms (28ins). Weight, minimum weight over eighteen months: dogs 54 kgs (120lbs); bitches 46 kgs (100lbs).

FAULTS: Any departure from the foregoing points should be considered a fault and the seriousness with which the fault should be regarded should be in exact proportion to its degree.

NOTE: Male animals should have two apparently normal testicles fully descended into the scrotum.

Reproduced by kind permission of the English Kennel Club.

AMERICAN BREED STANDARD

GENERAL APPEARANCE

The Great Dane combines, in its regal appearance, dignity, strength and elegance with great size and a powerful, well-formed, smoothly muscled body. It is one of the giant breeds, but is unique in that its general conformation must be so well balanced that it never appears clumsy, and shall move with a long reach and powerful drive, it is always a unit – the Apollo of dogs. A Great Dane must be spirited, courageous, never timid; always friendly and dependable. This physical and mental combination is the characteristic which gives the Great Dane the majesty possessed by no other breed. It is particularly true of this breed that there is an impression of great masculinity in dogs compared to an impression of femininity in bitches. Lack of true Dane breed type, as defined in this standard, is a serious fault.

SIZE, PROPORTION, SUBSTANCE
The male should appear more massive throughout than the bitch, with larger frame and heavier bone. In the ratio between length and height, the Great Dane should be square. In bitches, a somewhat longer body is permissible, providing she is well proportioned to her height. Coarseness or lack of substance are equally undesirable. The male shall not be less than 30 inches at the shoulders, but it is preferable that he is 32 inches or more, providing he is well proportioned to his height. The female shall not be less than 28 inches at the shoulders, but it is preferable that she be 30 inches or more, providing she is well proportioned to her height. Danes under minimum height must be disqualified.

HEAD – The head shall be rectangular, long, distinguished, finely chiseled, especially below the eyes. Seen from the side, the Dane's forehead must be sharply set off from the bridge of the nose (a strongly pronounced stop). The plane of the skull and the plane of the muzzle must be straight and parallel to one another. The skull plane under and to the inner point of the eyes must slope without any bony protuberance in a smooth line to a full square jaw with a deep muzzle (fluttering lips are undesirable). The masculinity of the male is very pronounced in structural appearance of the head. The bitch's head is more delicately formed.

Seen from the top, the skull should have parallel sides and the bridge of the nose should be as broad as possible. The cheek muscles should not be prominent. The length from the tip of the nose to the center of the stop should be equal to the length from the center of the stop to the rear of the slightly developed occiput. The head should be angular from all sides and should have flat planes with dimensions in proportion to the size of the Dane. Whiskers may be trimmed or left natural.

Eyes shall be medium size, deep set, and dark, with a lively intelligent expression. The eyelids are almond-shaped and relatively tight, with well developed brows. Haws and mongolian eyes are serious faults. In harlequins, the eyes should be dark; light colored eyes, eyes of different colors and wall eyes are permitted but not desirable.

Ears shall be high set, medium in size and of moderate thickness, folded forward close to the cheek. The top line of the folded ear should be level with the skull. If cropped, the ear length is in proportion to the size of the head and the ears are carried uniformly erect.

Nose shall be black, except in the blue Dane, where it is a dark blue-black. A black spotted nose is permitted on the harlequin; a pink colored nose is not desirable. A split nose is a disqualification.

Teeth shall be strong, well developed, clean and with full dentition. The incisors of the lower jaw touch very lightly the bottoms of the inner surface of the upper incisors (scissors bite). An undershot jaw is a very serious fault. Overshot or wry bites are serious faults. Even bites, misaligned or crowded incisors are minor faults.

NECK, TOPLINE, BODY – The neck shall be firm, high set, well arched, long and muscular. From the nape, it should gradually broaden and flow smoothly into the withers. The neck underline should be clean. Withers shall slope smoothly into a short level back with a broad loin. The chest shall be broad, deep and well muscled. The forechest should be well developed without a pronounced sternum. The brisket extends to the elbow, with well sprung ribs. The body underline should be tightly muscled with a well-defined tuck-up. The croup should be broad and very slightly sloping The tail should be set high and smoothly into the croup, but not quite level with the back, a continuation of the spine. The tail should be broad at the base, tapering uniformly down to the hock joint. At rest, the tail should fall straight. When excited or running, it may curve slightly, but never above the level of the back. A ring or hooked tail is a serious fault. A docked tail is a disqualification.

FOREQUARTERS – The forequarters, viewed from the side, shall be strong and muscular. The shoulder blade must be strong and sloping, forming, as near as possible, a right angle in its articulation with the upper arm. A line from the upper tip of the shoulder to the back of the elbow joint should be perpendicular. The ligaments and muscles holding the shoulder blade to the rib cage must be well developed, firm and securely attached to prevent loose shoulders. The shoulder blade and the upper arm should be the same length. The elbow should be one-half the distance from the withers to the ground. The strong pasterns should slope slightly. The feet should be round and compact with well arched toes, neither toeing in, toeing out, nor rolling to the inside or outside. The nails should be short, strong and as dark as possible, except that they may be lighter in harlequins. Dewclaws may or may not be removed.

HINDQUARTERS – The hindquarters shall be strong, broad, muscular and well angulated, with well let down hocks. Seen from the rear, the hock joints appear to be perfectly straight, turned neither toward the inside nor toward the outside. The rear feet should be round and compact, with well-arched toes, neither toeing in nor out. The nails should be short, strong and as dark as possible, except they may be lighter in harlequins. Wolf claws are a serious fault.

COAT – The coat shall be short, thick and clean with a smooth glossy appearance.

COLOR, MARKINGS AND PATTERN
Brindle – The base color shall be yellow gold and always brindled with strong black cross stripes in a chevron pattern. A black mask is preferred. Black should appear on the eye rims and eyebrows, and may appear on the ears and tail tip. The more intensive the base color and the more distinct and even the brindling, the more preferred will be the color. Too much or too little brindling are equally undesirable. White markings at the chest and toes, black-fronted, dirty colored brindles are not desirable.

Fawn – The color shall be yellow gold with a black mask. Black should appear on the eye rims and eyebrows, and may appear on the ears and tail tip. The deep yellow gold must always be given the preference. White markings at the chest and toes, black-fronted dirty colored fawns are not desirable.

Blue – The color shall be a pure steel blue. White markings at the chest and toes are not desirable.

Black – The color shall be a glossy black. White markings at the chest and toes are not desirable

Harlequin – Base color shall be pure white with black torn patches irregularly and well distributed over the entire body; a pure white neck is preferred. The black patches should never be large enough to give the appearance of a blanket, nor so small as to give a stippled or dappled effect. Eligible, but less desirable, are a few small gray patches, or a white base with single black hairs showing through, which tend to give a salt and pepper or dirty effect.

Any variance in color or markings as described above shall be faulted to the extent of the deviation. Any Great Dane which does not fall within the above color classifications must be disqualified.

GAIT – The gait denotes strength and power with long, easy strides resulting in no tossing, rolling or bouncing of the topline or body. The backline shall appear level and parallel to the ground. The long reach should strike the ground below the nose while the head is carried forward. The powerful rear drive should be balanced to the reach. As speed increases, there is a natural tendency for the legs to converge toward the centerline of balance beneath the body. There should be no twisting in or out at the elbow or hock joints.

TEMPERAMENT – The Great Dane must be spirited, courageous, always friendly and dependable, and never timid or aggressive.

DISQUALIFICATIONS
Danes under minimum height.
Split nose.
Docked tail.
Any color other than those described under "Color, Markings and Patterns".
Reproduced by kind permission of the American Kennel Club.
Approved September 11, 1990.

THE BREED STANDARD DISCUSSED

If we accept that the breed Standard is a word picture, a black and white description of the breed, necessarily short and succinct, basic and accurate, then here we have the blueprint for our breed. Our depth of interest is such that we would like to know more. This is why we read everything we can lay our hands on, seek information from those who know more

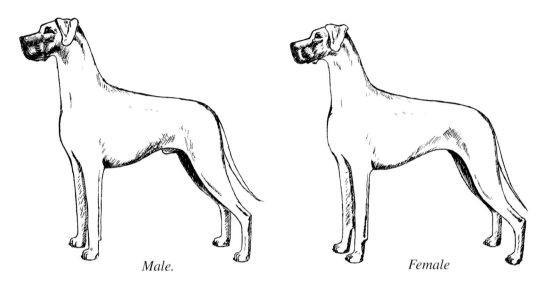

Male.   *Female*

*These Great Danes both correspond to the Breed Standard: Strength
with elegance and a look of dash and daring.*

about the breed than we do, exchange theories and ideas with our peers and generally throw ourselves into a learning process about our chosen breed.

The black and white word picture that is the breed Standard gradually takes on texture, depth and detail as we come to know and understand the breed points. It is the knowledge and experience gained over many years that brings the Standard to life for us – and in glorious technicolour – if our will to learn is great enough. Instead of wanting to change the Standard to fit the dogs we have, we will strive to breed Danes to fit the Standard.

GENERAL APPEARANCE
This is a most descriptive paragraph. The balance of strength with elegance is what gives the Great Dane such nobility; that, coupled with the proud head carriage, correct expression and clean flowing outline. Please note the British Standard asks for "a *look* of dash and daring, of being ready to go anywhere and do anything". This means *a look!* A Dane actually *behaves* with dignity.

The explanation comes under the heading 'Characteristics' in the British Standard, and it is encompassed in the 'General Appearance' paragraph in the German and American Standards. The alert expression gives the *look* but standing or moving, dignity is shown. The word 'powerful' is used to echo the 'strongly' for those who may be lingering over the 'elegance' to the cost of the Great Dane's remarkable size and substance. The word 'majestic' or 'majesty' encapsulates the appearance and demeanour of the breed and brings us closer to understanding true breed type.

Type is what makes one breed recognisable from another. For many years, I confess, I thought type came from head and expression. I now understand that, to be truly typical, a Dane must be typical in all departments. If any part of a Dane reminds you of some other breed, then that Dane is untypical. If the Dane has such elegance that 'greyhoundy' springs to mind – that Dane is untypical. If the Dane has such power and substance that the word 'Mastiffy' is on your lips – that Dane is untypical.

It is the correct blending of the Breed Standard requirements – the overall balance and outline, the flow of one part into another, the proportions, the carriage, the nobility and the majesty that gives us our Great Dane.

TEMPERAMENT

The Standard can only generalise; it is not attempting to describe the personality of a Dane, just the temperament or attitude as displayed, whether in a normal day-to-day situation or in the show ring."Kindly without nervousness, friendly and outgoing" (British Standard), "friendly and dependable, and never timid or aggressive" (American Standard), "friendly, loving and affectionate" (German Standard). A Dane is kind; they are certainly not unkind, spiteful or aggressive without provocation. There is a gentleness about our breed but not nervousness, which would suggest a cringing, frightened, unstable attitude. A "friendly" dog describes 'normal' dog behaviour. Dogs *like* people. Although we see our breed as something special, Danes are just dogs, who should show normal behaviour, reasonable behaviour – with dignity!

HEAD AND SKULL

For me, much of the Dane's beauty and appeal comes from the head and expression. Dane devotees will be heard talking lovingly of parallel planes, length of foreface, clean skulls

Endroma Miss Ebony: Heady study of a Great Dane, British Style.

Diane Pearce.

Am. Ch. Mountdania's Ashley: A stunning head study of a Great Dane with cropped ears – which is a requirement in the American and German Breed Standards.

and drop of lip. I think it is fair to say that, by and large, heads are of a good standard. We do not see many snipy forefaces or heavy backskulls, but I think we must watch the tendency towards excessive 'drop of lip', which is just that, 'lips' without the strength of jaw or muzzle.

EYES

Shape, size and colour contribute to the essential 'expression' so important in the breed. It can be argued that 'light' eyes are only a cosmetic fault and therefore not as important as a constructional point. I can sympathise with this view as long as the 'lightness' of eye does not mar the expression. A light eye can give a spiteful look which is, of course, completely foreign to the breed. I have known Danes with lightish eyes that did not offend, as the gentle, kind, quizzical expression was retained. There is some leeway between "preferably dark" and eyes like yellow headlamps!

EARS

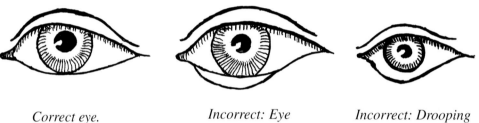

Correct eye.   *Incorrect: Eye showing haw.*   *Incorrect: Drooping bottom lid.*

This is obviously a point of difference, with both the American and German Standards asking for cropped ears, while the British Standard stipulates "Triangular, medium size, set high on skull and folded forward, not pendulous". In the British Dane the size and the set of the ears are essential in order to achieve the "alert expression". Huge ears hanging down the side of the head give a doleful look that is anything but typical. The high set is equally important to cropped ears; they should not be too far apart and the size (medium) should be in proportion to the shape of the head.

MOUTH

Again the Standard is explicit. The breed is required to have a scissor bite with the teeth level. An incorrect mouth, to any degree from misplaced, twisted teeth to half-inch undershot, is referred to as a 'bad' mouth by those in the breed – one of the most emotive problems and one of the most heartbreaking for an enthusiastic showgoer or breeder.

A bad mouth, which means a mouth less than perfect, is sometimes referred to as 'a hidden fault', i.e. it is not noticeable until the lips are actually lifted or parted and the teeth examined. Those wishing to minimise the importance of an incorrect mouth will use the

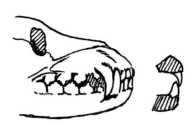

Correct: Scissor bite.

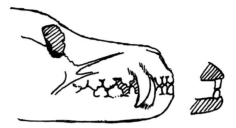

Incorrect: Level bite.

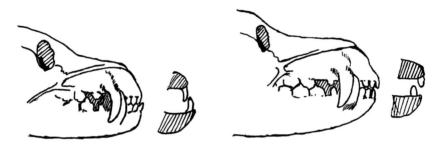

Incorrect:
Undershot mouth.

Incorrect:
Overshot mouth.

argument that "a Dane does not walk on its teeth", therefore it cannot be taken as seriously as a constructional fault. They will tell you that it does not stop the Dane from eating perfectly well. They will use the old chestnut that "it is only *one* fault".

Those to whom a bad mouth is unforgivable – admirable perhaps if their attitude was equally severe to any and every other area of the Breed Standard and any divergence from same – will maintain that a bad mouth is more serious because it is a 'hidden' fault. We must also see that logic. Incorrect mouths are certainly hereditary, and if bred from will occur and re-occur for generations with distressing regularity.

Referring to mouths, I have used the words 'emotive' and 'distressing'; if that gives the impression I am soft-pedalling on this subject, that is not so at all. The mouth must be correct. It can be considered somewhat unfair that a bad mouth – so obvious once anyone looks at the teeth – that it is often an immediate disqualification from any wins in the show ring – whereas any or all of the other faults that occur in this or any other breed can go undetected by those with insufficient knowledge. We even read, in critiques, faults praised

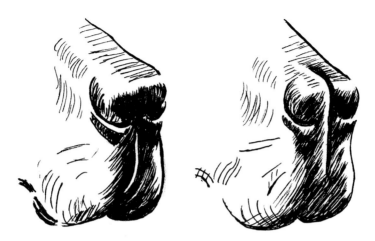

Correct: Nose showing
characteristic ridge.

Incorrect: Split nose.

as virtues by judges who do not understand basic construction.

However, the bad mouth cannot escape detection. Please do not try to delude yourself that the jawline is right, it is just the teeth that are situated badly. Any excuse you can manufacture, with the best will in the world, really will not help. To attempt to breed with a Great Dane with a bad mouth is, in my opinion, bordering on the criminal. No matter how good the dog is in every other respect, bad mouths will appear in that Dane's offspring, and in their offspring – and on and on!

NECK

A long, crested neck helps give the Dane the regal appearance so sought after. The neck should be clean and free from loose skin; the junction of head and neck should be well defined. The neck is beautifully described, as long as we read 'long' as 'long'; *not* 'the longer the better'! *The length of neck should be in proportion to the overall Great Dane.* We are discussing Great Danes not Giraffes. There is no virtue in having the longest neck in the world if it has made the Dane appear unbalanced and out of proportion.

It is required for the junction of head and neck to be well defined in order to help that 'well arched' neck, so typical of the breed. A good Great Dane with the correct temperament *uses* the neck to its best advantage to accentuate the beautiful crested appearance, turning its head from one side to another to view quizzically whatever has caught the attention. If it happens to be a judge who loves the breed that is the object of your Dane's interest, you are halfway home, as a Dane displaying a crested neck with such expression is quite irresistible.

In all honesty, a favourite Dane, Ch. Dicarl The Heavyweight, did not have the longest neck, but it was beautifully crested, and he used his adequate length of neck to such advantage that any lack of length was rarely commented upon. A short neck can make the Dane appear stuffy and thereby lacking elegance. The neck should be free from loose skin; if the neck is not clean, the Dane is 'throaty'.

Confession time! I had my problems with this part of the breed Standard. In my early years, Muriel Osborne, doyen of the breed of the Blendon prefix, said to me one day: "You are breeding some very good Danes, Mrs Johnson; you are having and will continue to have great success, and deservedly so. But there are two problems in your Danes, two faults you don't take seriously enough because you consider them minor faults. You must watch throat and feet in your line." How wise she was (we will deal with feet in due course). She was absolutely right, of course: I convinced myself that a bit of loose throat was a small price to pay for a magnificent head on a strong, muscular, crested neck.

FOREQUARTERS

The Standard's first words in the first paragraph under 'General Appearance' are "very muscular", and the American Standard describes a "powerful, well-formed, smoothly muscled body"; so we should, therefore, have the word 'muscular' firmly in our minds. The British Standard asks for "muscular shoulder"; the American Standard stipulates "strong and muscular" forequarters.

The shoulders should not be loaded; they must be well sloped back. This deals with the incorrect coarse, bumpy, heavy shoulder, which makes the front too wide, prohibiting the elbows from sitting correctly, i.e. 'loaded', and with the upright shoulder and steep upper

Correct front.

Incorrect: Elbows out and front pinning in.

Incorrect: Tied in elbow and front, feet turning out. In a puppy this 'ten-to-two' front may improve.

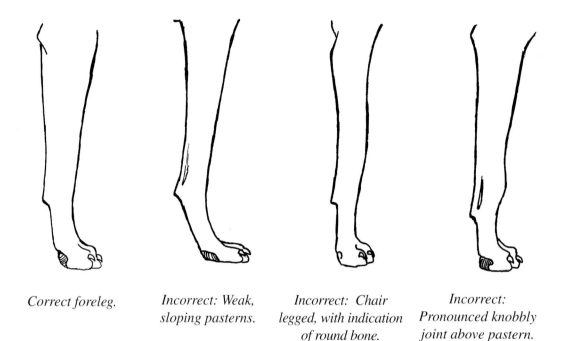

Correct foreleg. *Incorrect: Weak, sloping pasterns.* *Incorrect: Chair legged, with indication of round bone.* *Incorrect: Pronounced knobbly joint above pastern.*

arm, which causes a very upright neck and head carriage, considered 'smart' and 'showy' by those lacking understanding of correctly laid shoulders.

Shoulders are perhaps the most difficult part of anatomy to grasp – I shudder to think how irritating I must have been to senior breeders trying to educate me about the breed! I well remember Nellie Ennals (Bringtonhill), another doyen, sitting all one evening surrounded by photographs and sketches, trying to explain shoulders to me. Nell, who is a very calm and mild-mannered lady, finally lost her patience as the midnight hour approached and exploded with: "Di, I don't think you will *ever* understand shoulders!"

I still think shoulders are difficult to understand or describe with the written word. You need to work at it, with live models, with the eyes and hands, and with time and experience in the breed. If shoulders are easy to understand, why do so many judges write "good shoulders" when referring to Danes that are totally incorrect in that department?

Elbows must be well under the body, which gives freedom of forehand and correct movement. Generally, the British Breed Standard is extremely descriptive and well written; however, there is no mention of forechest specifically, and we must assume that the correct forehand assembly, with the correct brisket, will give the correct forechest. The American Standard is more explicit and stipulates "The chest shall be broad, deep and well-muscled. The forechest should be well developed without a pronounced sternum." For a Great Dane to be pigeon-chested has always been recognised as a fault, and we now see too many Danes with enormous over-developed forechests and loaded shoulders accentuated by short forelegs. The Dane immediately loses elegance of outline and grace of form, not to mention balance. Forelegs should be perfectly straight with big flat bone. A Dane that is absolutely true in front is a joy to behold. The Standard tells us quite clearly what is required. In my opinion, bone is bred in; sadly, over-zealous rearing can sometimes cause round bone and knuckling over at pastern joints.

BODY

A deep brisket is required, reaching the elbows. Ribs must be well sprung; but not below elbows, which would give a 'stumpy' look, and not slab-sided, which would give a 'narrow' look to the body. Strength is again referred to in the back and loins, in both the German and British Standards, so obviously a topline that dips is incorrect. Too long a back will sag and ruin the correct proportions and balance of a Dane.

The American Standard states: "The body underline should be tightly muscled with a well-defined tuck up." The belly should be well drawn up and the loins slightly arched, giving the grace of form; the operative word is 'slightly', never bordering on the 'whippety'; but without the tuck up and with an 'ironing board' flat topline, the Dane would appear 'cloddy', lacking elegance of outline.

HINDQUARTERS

Again, strength and muscularity are emphasised in all three Standards. The second thigh should be long and well developed or well angulated, again accentuating elegance of outline and the need for length of legs to give balance. There should be good turn of stifle, and this means quite simply that the stifle must not be straight and it must not be over-angulated!

When studying the Standard, we must use all the information given in all parts therein. It is the individual parts that make the whole. It will serve no useful purpose to be obtuse or pedantic. Those studying the Breed Standard cannot get this far without having acquired an overall picture of the type of dog we are looking for.

A straight stifle would give the Dane a stilted look; the Dane would be completely unbalanced, as we have already ascertained that the forequarters have 'good' angulation, so its back end would be at odds with its front half, wouldn't it? Commonsense? I think so.

An over-angulated stifle can be taken care of with similar reasoning. I suggest there is some leeway with the 'good turn of stifle'. What some describe as 'adequate', others will find lacking in hind-angulation. Others will enthuse over 'excellent' hind angulation which may be one step past 'good' for some. What is 'good'? Enough, but not too much? It is the hindquarters that provide the propulsion, i.e. where the drive comes from on the move. The hocks must be set low, turning neither in nor out. Weakness in the hindquarters can be a temporary stage in a young Dane's growth. While lacking maturity and awaiting muscle to develop, the youngster can appear cow-hocked – an alarming and unattractive picture that must never be seen in an adult Dane.

FEET

The feet should be round and compact – cat-like! I have already admitted I found the ideal foot easier to understand than to achieve. I still maintain that it is easier to get a wonderful cat-like foot on a Dane that is under-boned, but I also admit that the true and correct foot is a most attractive, not to mention necessary, feature. I was so obsessed by strong heavy bone, I often forgave a less than perfect foot.

While I hope I have made it quite clear that the Standard must be taken with the utmost seriousness, I also believe that there is room for humour in all walks of life. Doyen of the Moonsfield Great Danes, Edna Harrild, once gave a dog of mine the CC with the comment: "Just be grateful that the grass in this show ring hadn't been mown properly, because it was so long I couldn't get a good look at his feet!"

Toe nails are preferably dark, except in harlequins.

TAIL
An incorrectly set on or carried tail can ruin the overall picture of the Dane. We are looking for elegance of outline and grace of form, so surely the tail must be a continuation of the flowing lines. If the tail has a 'stuck on as an afterthought' appearance, if the tail carriage deviates from that described in the Standard, then the 'flow' is interrupted at great cost to the outline of the breed.

GAIT/MOVEMENT
The British Standard asks for movement to be "lithe, springy and free"; the American Standard describes "long, easy strides", and the German Standard stipulates "fleeting, stepping out". So we cannot possibly interpret this to encompass heavy, plodding or short-striding constricted gait. A Dane should cover the ground well, showing a length of stride with good reach in front and plenty of drive in the rear, as we already have established from the 'drive from hocks'. Remembering words like 'majestic' and 'nobility', we will understand that the head should be carried high and proudly. The aim is for "majestic action displaying dignity". What a dream – if only....

The expression 'moved well' is used when the Dane has managed to get to one end of the ring and back again without falling over! Nobody ever said it was easy to achieve the desired movement; to breed the ideal construction; to build the correct muscle; to rear a Dane to the peak of physical fitness; to encourage and develop its personality so that the dog has the *will* to move as described. It is far from easy.

Based on the fact that I have probably only seen a dozen Danes in my whole life whose movement I would describe as approaching the ideal as required in the Breed Standard, I have to conclude that it is an extremely difficult feature to achieve.

COAT
There are not many problems in understanding or achieving the desired quality of coat. The Dane's general health and condition will show in the coat, and Danes that live in outdoor kennels may develop a slightly thicker coat in winter months or extreme cold. Moulting times can be very difficult, especially in youngsters, sometimes giving a positively 'moth-eaten' look to the coat. Correct feeding, some grooming, and time, will solve those problems.

COLOUR

We can choose the colour of Dane we wish to own or breed; that is our prerogative – we choose the colour that appeals to us. When judging, we are judging Great Danes! We must, therefore, never allow a colour preference to influence our decisions, as long as that colour is allowed within the Breed Standard.

BRINDLE

I find the on-going discussion about number and positioning of stripes quite wearying. How can we expect the Standard to specify there should be 34, 87 or 129 stripes? Some think the stripes should completely circle the body. Some maintain that if a Dane has just three stripes on only one side of the body, it can be considered correct. The British Standard states "must be striped". It does not say well-striped or evenly striped; but if it did, the words 'well' and 'evenly' would probably be up for discussion! Surely, this is another case for using our commonsense. The American Standard is more explicit, stating "strong, black cross stripes in a chevron pattern", and the German Standard asks for "well-defined black stripes". Ground colour should be as in fawns.

FAWN

The British Standard gives "lightest buff to deepest orange" as a permitted colour range for fawns; the German Standard describes "fawn-golden and fawn to dark golden fawn", with golden fawn as the preferred colour, whereas the American Standard restricts itself to "yellow gold". The precise shade of colour is hard to define. For instance, how do we see buff in its lightest hue? Well, I do not see it as the dingy, dish-watery colour grey that some seem to find so attractive. But then, my favourite colour is what I consider to be deepest orange, which others perceive as being too dark.

I find the dark shadings on head and ears greatly enhancing, and that is in order according to all three Standards. The British Standard states they are "acceptable"; the German Standard states that a dark mask is desired, whereas the American Standard specifically asks for fawns to be "yellow gold with a black mask".

BLUE

Both the German and the American Standard require this colour to be a pure steel blue. The British Standards gives more scope with "light grey to deep slate".

BLACK

Black is black, and there is no argument on this subject!

In all colours, white is only permissible on chest and feet, but it is not desirable even there. That is very fair: we do not *want* white on Danes, but the Standard is sensibly avoiding a 'throwing the baby out with the bath water' situation. A Dane of great quality overall should not be dismissed because of some white on chest or feet. Is not the Standard once more leaving room for commonsense? The American standard states that "white markings at the chest and toes are not desirable"; the German Standard allows a small amount of white marking, but is is quite clear that excessive white markings will be penalised.

HARLEQUIN
The written words of the breed Standard describe this colour very well. As with most things in life, it is easier said than done. Harlequin is, without doubt, the most difficult of the colours. A correctly marked harlequin with pure white background is a spectacular and beautiful sight. An incorrectly marked Harlequin with merle flecking cannot be seen to fit the breed Standard.

WEIGHT AND SIZE
The British Standard gives minimum height and weight requirements; the American and German Standards restrict themselves to height minimums only. These are easily achieved by today's Great Danes, and greatly surpassed! For as long as I can remember there has been a clamouring in some quarters for the minimum height to be raised. I would guess that the average male Dane in the show ring stands 35 ins at the withers and bitches probably 33 ins.

   Height is not a virtue; it is not a case of 'the bigger the better' or 'the taller the better'. The British Standard does not say a male Great Dane *should* be 30 ins; it surely says he should not be "less than 30". The American Standard is more specific, stating "The male should not be less than 30 inches at the shoulder, but it is preferable that he be 32 inches or more, providing he is well proportioned to his height." For some it is not a realistic height, as all of today's Danes tower so loftily above it. Food for thought!

THINKING ABOUT THE BREED STANDARD
Knowing the breed Standard by heart and being able to recite it parrot-fashion, as in schooldays with multiplication tables, does not mean a thing! We must feel and think about the words and what they mean – we must respect the Breed Standard.

   Before most of us were born, the late Mrs T.F. Booker wrote the following verse about the Great Dane, emphasising the points of the breed Standard:-

If you would own a winning Dane.
These points about him please retain.
He must be full of dash and dare
Do anything – go anywhere.
He must be big and sound and strong.
A timid, creepy Dane's all wrong.
Whate'er his colour, he must be
Brilliantly marked, not dingily.
He must not have a perky face
But air of dignity and grace.
His eyes not prominent or light,
But clever, quizzical and bright.
His nose, full, broad and with a ridge,
Most typical – above the bridge.

He must not have an ugly lump.
Above his brow like camel's hump.
A lack of stop, or mean "down face"
And snipy muzzle's a disgrace.
His crested neck he carries high
And holds his head up to the sky.
A dippy back's outside the Pale,
And cut-off croup and low set tail.
Straight stifles are a bad fault too.
Steep shoulders he must then eschew.
Aim for nobility and grace –
A King of Dogs, with regal face,
Who with his life will you defend
And ever be your faithful friend.

Chapter Four

THE SHOW RING

A Great Dane is a dog to be proud of; a dog with tremendous aesthetic appeal. Your daily exercise will be interrupted by people, wanting to admire your Dane. Along with the corny "Why don't you put a saddle on and ride him?" and "I bet he costs a fortune to feed" will come "You ought to show him!"

TO SHOW OR NOT TO SHOW
If you purchased your puppy from an established show kennel, the breeder will probably want you to show, and offer help and encouragement. The Dane is a comparatively easy dog to show, as grooming is minimal, a wipe over with a damp chamois leather and a polish with a piece of velvet will keep your Dane looking well, provided, of course, good muscular condition is maintained. Showing your Dane can be a wonderful interest and hobby; you will meet people from all walks of life who share the interest with you, and friendships will be forged that will last your lifetime. It is necessary for a proviso to be added here. Showing your Dane can be great fun, *provided* you have the temperament for the sport! If your love and regard for your Dane will remain constant, regardless of success or failure in the show ring, then by all means enter the show world, share the pleasure of the day out with your Dane, rejoice in the wins and accept the losses. Remember, you are showing for *fun*, there are no financial rewards – just a little prestige; and a fistful of red cards, or even a title, will not make your Dane a better companion or a truer friend.

Showing is an expensive and time-consuming pastime, and if you do get bitten by the show bug then the dog scene will become a way of life. Having spent thirty glorious, heady years riding the roundabout, I can thoroughly recommend the hobby; but then I did, perhaps, have more than my fair share of winning – eventually!

APPRENTICESHIP
A great asset to those who wish to show their dog, is to learn to lose, preferably before you acquire the taste for winning. To gain the odd prize card gives encouragement and spurs you on to greater ambition. Too much success too soon, although enjoyable at the time, denies you the benefits of the apprenticeship served over years of striving, coping with disappointments and, hopefully, disregarding the rose-coloured spectacles through which we

The joy of a third CC – only the Dane Champion seems unimpressed! For Frances and Jack Krall it was a dream come true, especially when the judge was Edna Harrild of Moonsfield fame.

Winning in America is a very glamorous affair. This beautiful Great Dane bitch is Champion Rojons Rumour Has It.

To win the Group at Crufts was a fitting climax of young Shaun MacAlpine's handling career. Shaun's dedication to the breed began as a small boy and continued to grow, showing the potential to be one of the breed's top handlers. His life sadly ended at the age of 21 years. The judge was Mrs Marion Fairbrother, and Sir Dudley Forward appears to be admiring Shaun's handling of Ch. Dicarl Tendellie.

Clark.

all, understandably, see our own much-loved Danes.

It was ten long years before one of our Danes won a Challenge Certificate. During those ten years, we learnt. By going to shows and watching the best Danes, studying the judging, discussing the placings with those more knowledgeable and experienced, by grasping true breed type and excellence, we learnt to appreciate the breed and to understand just why our 'Domonic' did not win CCs or why our 'Rosie' did not gain her title.

While we adored our own Danes, we learnt to see the virtues of other people's Danes also, and to accept – albeit with disappointment – when ours were beaten by better specimens. Can you do this? It is not always easy. It is more satisfying to complain that the judge is an idiot – or crooked – or both! Exhibiting will bring out the best and the worst in people. We all go to shows hoping to win, but if at the end of a losing day you can be so disgruntled that it affects the enjoyment that should be shared by you and your Dane, then you should ask yourself if you really have the temperament to be showing your Great Dane.

RING TRAINING

If you have bred or bought a promising puppy with showing in mind and you have reared the pup to the very best of your ability, you will probably be longing to get your puppy into the show ring. You will be well advised to remember that a day at a dog show is a long and tiring one for a Dane baby. The puppy will sleep for a couple of days after a show. It is never wise to over-show a baby. They are developing and growing in the puppy months, and any undue stress or exhaustion will arrest their development.

Teaching the puppy to stand and trot for suitable lengths of time must be made enjoyable. Ask a friend to gently 'go over' the pup, to look at the teeth, to attract the puppy's attention and encourage correct use of neck and ears, and to generally persuade the pup that the judging process is pleasant.

Local classes that specialise in ring training are invaluable, but again, do not overdo it. Puppies easily become bored, so resist the temptation of trying to turn an interested baby into a little showing robot.

HANDLING YOUR DANE

Good handling is making your Dane look the very best, and to do that you need to understand your Dane's construction. You must know and maximise virtues, and recognise and minimise failings. You must learn the most natural and attractive stance, study movement and find the optimum speed, and develop some knack of getting your Dane's attention in order to show some 'sparkle' at the crucial time.

As I have already acknowledged, along with many judges in critiques over the years, my husband, Carl, was an exceptional handler of Great Danes. He was a natural, an extrovert with a confident 'showy' style that could hardly be overlooked. There are different styles of handling, and I often preferred the quieter, gentler style of Peter Russell of the Endroma Great Danes, but Carl was my handler – and I could not have asked for a more effective one.

Carl showed little interest in puppies in the first three or four months of their lives; it was only when I told him that *this* was a good one, that his adrenalin started to flow. At about four and a half months, he would begin to build a rapport with a promising show puppy,

My husband, the handler! Carl Johnson showing exactly how it is done with Ch. She's Sophie of Dicarl.

*It takes time,
patience and
dedication to become
a good handler.*

Diane Pearce.

*Maggi Down gently
teaching a most
promising baby
Dane, Cheney Truly
Scrumptious, to find
her correct show
stance.*

spending time most days to teach the puppy the art of showing. Puppies learn quickly, and when they saw Carl coming with their 'show lead' as opposed to any old exercise lead, their attitude would change: they were learning to enjoy being show dogs.

I can remember sometimes being quite saddened by a five-month-old baby behaving so perfectly and standing so correctly on the lead, and I would urge the lesson to an end for the joy of seeing the puppy charge about, acting silly. Our Danes knew the difference between playtime and showtime, and they enjoyed the latter just as much as the former. A Dane in the show ring is well aware of the winning, and most of them love applause and glory. Just think about any Dane taking a lap of honour after a big win – don't they show off?

Carl worked on the theory that all dogs need individual handling: the trick is to find the best way to show each dog.

STYLES OF HANDLING

LOOSE LEADING: In my perfect world, all Danes would be shown on a loose lead, naturally, alert, displaying nobility. Bill Siggers was a master at this art. With the flat of his hand gently on a Dane's neck, he could help the dog find its true balance and look its very

A young Champion, The Contender of Dicarl, did not need stringing. Both dog and handler are enjoying themselves – and the result is still impressive.

Diane Pearce

Champion Dicarl The Alliance with Algwynne standing proudly at the end of a loose lead, showing natural dignity and balance with flowing outline.

Thomas Fall.

best. A Dane full of self-importance and with an interest in the surrounding world, will show this way and never fail to command attention. Of course, a Dane is always moved on a loose lead, but sometimes when standing a dog will need a little more involvement by the handler.

BAITING: This technique is sometimes used. Many, many pounds of liver have been baked in my kitchen when Carl was campaigning a Dane who needed an added incentive to show to the best advantage. Jeff Luscott of the Jalus Great Danes was an expert at this style, standing in front of the Dane tempting it with edible treats. This works well with a greedy Dane, or if the tidbit is thrown about it will attract the attention of a nosey Dane. Perhaps the latter method is not to be encouraged as it can distract other Danes in the ring; in fact, it can sometimes help the opposition if they are equally inquisitive.

STRINGING: For control of their charges, slick handlers assure us there is nothing as effective as stringing. It is now universally accepted as 'the' way to handle a Dane – more's the pity. It certainly gives a smart outline; it is certainly a way of disguising 'loose throats' and controlling ear placement. The Dane is 'stacked' by the handler and each leg is positioned to the handler's liking. I do not know why handlers feel it necessary to reposition each of the four legs – one of them must have been in a reasonable position, surely?

   As you can probably tell, I yearn for the days when handlers simply walked the Dane around them until they walked into their natural balanced stance! Doyen of the breed, Ulla Magnusson of the Swedish Airways Great Dane kennel, could string a Dane beautifully,

Handlers should look smart and convince their dog that he is something special – fully achieved by Tony Pearce with Ch. Anset The Smoothie.

Rosern.

Sometimes there are two good handlers in the same family: here Helen Pearce demonstrates her style with Ch. Anset The Sorceror.

Ch. Endroma Morgan's Boy showing just what an extrovert character he was, taking all of Peter Russell's expertise as a handler. I can't think of another kennel to breed Champions in four of the five colours. This was achieved by Endroma, and Peter was always the man on the end of the lead.

This clever exhibitor with stylish Great Dane ably illustrates the old 'handler's maxim' – one eye on the dog and the other on the judge

allowing the Dane to retain presence and nobility. Carl was quick to copy this and most exhibitors followed suit, but not always with the finesse and understanding of the originators. Too often, nowadays, we see a ring full of static, strangled Danes with neck stretched up at a most unnatural angle. What is worse, they attempt to move them while 'strung'!

MOVING YOUR DANE

Always move your Dane on a loose lead in the show ring. The Dane should be taught to move up and down, in a triangle, and to circle the ring, depending on what the judge asks for. Every Dane has a comfortable pace to show the best movement; moving too fast or too slow will highlight movement faults. A good handler will watch a friend move his Dane and assess the optimum speed. Perhaps more slowly, going away, will give the dog a little more let-down in hock, aiding the desired drive, while a brisker coming-back movement may 'tidy' a lazy front.

Should the Dane have a pacing habit, i.e. moving both legs on the same side in unison, a smart tug under the chin with the lead should break the rhythm and upset the balance into the correct action.

HANDLER'S ATTITUDE

Many handlers have asked and still do ask Carl for secrets of success as a handler. If it were possible to 'tell how', I know he would. Handlers, whatever the breed, are a race apart; they share a common bond, a will to win, a fascination with the art. Carl admired Olive Davies of the Oldmanor Great Danes in his early days for her attitude, and he developed similar dedication and understanding of his charges. A handler needs to believe in his dog, and together they will do the job to the best of their ability.

A handler has to concentrate and draw the judge's eye to the best features, e.g. if the Dane has a beautiful crested neck, then gently stroke the neck. A gun-barrel front with wonderful bone should be pointed at the judge. A beautiful flowing outline should be displayed in profile. Conversely, if the Dane is a little long cast, then the dog is always shown three-quarters on. If the eyes are slightly light, that Dane is never shown facing the sun or glaring at the judge. Never fidget with the part that fails; hand movements will pull the judge's eyes to the less than pleasing area.

A fit and happy Dane looks and shows well; the handler makes the outing enjoyable for both of them. Carl believes that a confident handler makes a confident exhibit, and he would never allow himself to show uncertainty or annoyance, as he is sure that a bad attitude goes down the lead from handler to Dane. A good handler should always be smart and sporting. Carl's maxim is: Good handlers make mediocre dogs look good, and make good dogs look great. But it is great dogs that make handlers.

Chapter Five

JUDGING GREAT DANES

THE JUDGE'S ROLE

Judging should never be undertaken lightly. It should never be considered an entitlement because you have shown a Dane for a couple of years. After an apprenticeship of many years spent learning about the breed from senior breeders, from the many excellent books and videos available, from seminars and teach-ins, and from a deep and genuine interest in dogs, and Great Danes in particular, you should have a knowledge of the anatomy and a good understanding of the dog's moving parts and how they work. You will have learned to appreciate the virtues that, when combined, produce a good, typical Great Dane, rather than indulging in the ringside critic's habits of fault spotting! This is a silly pastime, as any fool can spot faults, especially when armed with a catalogue and bolstered by companions lacking true understanding of the breed.

Fault judging is the road to nowhere. The perfect Great Dane has not yet been born, and you can rest assured it never will be. Every dog has faults in some area, to some degree. A good judge is aware of them and of their inevitability, but is in the middle of the ring to place the dogs in order of *merit*; this can only be achieved by looking for positives, not negatives. A judge is never asked to find the five *worst* dogs in the ring, but always to find the *best*. This can only be achieved by appreciating and recognising virtues, as described by the Breed Standard.

To be invited to judge the breed is certainly an honour, but more than that, it is a great responsibility. To judge is not compulsory and if you feel you are not yet ready for the responsibility, then by all means decline the offer and wait until such time as you feel able, not only to make balanced judgements, but to deal with the criticism and resentment that will undoubtedly follow your first appearance as a judge. Generally speaking, judges please the winners by confirming the owner's high opinion of their own dogs, and disappoint the losers who have an equally high opinion of *their* own dogs.

The trite belief that friends lost through judging were not friends in the first place may comfort in certain situations, and while a judge must never be influenced by the hurt feelings of exhibitors, it is courtesy to bear in mind that those entering dogs under you, all be it for your honest opinion, feel the same amount of love and pride in their Danes as you do for yours. A good judge should treat the losers with the same interest and respect as that

Jackie White of Tallbrook Great Dane fame, for many years a successful breeder and exhibitor in the USA, now an acclaimed judge of the breed. Jackie has been described as extremely knowledgeable, courteous, thorough, consistent and fair. All judges should aim for that sort of critique! Here Jackie awards BOB to the legendary and magnificent Ch. Von Shrado's I'm a Knockout. *Rinehart Photography.*

accorded to the winners. In any judge a little humility goes a long way. A quiet confidence must be displayed during the judging and during the post-mortems that will follow, should you allow. An inexperienced judge will not always have the authority and ability to terminate unwarranted comment, or the strength of character to survive the unpopularity that judging often brings.

Think, and think again before you agree to judge. Avoid the 'keeping up with the Joneses' syndrome – wanting to judge because 'she' has judged and been in the breed six months less than you have, or 'he' has judged and not done half as much winning as you. This all looks very petty when written down, but we all know that it happens. It is better to earn respect by

Jean Lanning of Clausentum Great Danes and author of several books on the breed, awarding a Group at Midland Counties Championship Show to a fawn bitch who loved the show ring, Champion Drumview Trade Secret.

John Hartley.

waiting until the senior breeders and judges urge you to begin judging because they feel your opinion may be of value. If you begin to judge too soon, you will regret it. Not only because of the tut-tutting "only been in the breed ten minutes" remark, but because you will display, in public, your lack of sufficient experience.

YOUR FIRST INVITATION TO JUDGE

Eventually, your first invitation to judge will arrive. Spend the months prior to the judging appointment wisely. It would be most unwise to tout for entries and to pass comments on the Danes currently being shown, as your ringside impressions can change drastically in the middle-of-the-ring, hands-on, situation. Speculation about what you will do 'on the day' will be rife. Try to avoid the trap of pre-judging, such as stating "I would never put up a Dane with light eyes," or "A Dane must have correct tail carriage to win under me." Instead, you must teach yourself to take a balanced view, disregarding your personal likes and dislikes, so that you can judge the Dane as a whole against the Breed Standard.

Remind yourself constantly that, whichever Danes compete for your assessment, you will judge them honestly and fairly 'on the day'. Dogs, just like people, have good and bad days. We all have days when we feel well and look good, other days we look our age and can't do a thing with our hair! No Dane 'shows like a bomb' and 'moves like a train' (whatever that means) on every outing, even though fond owners would have you believe that is the case.

Therefore, pre-judging your imagined entry alone or with 'friends', is really an awful waste of time. The one you have pegged for Best of Breed probably will not turn up, and the one you have not even considered, as he is always so dull and lacking showmanship, may have his day of days and display all the nobility and majesty you understand the breed is required to have, and so demand the BOB.

PRACTICALITIES OF JUDGING PROCEDURE

In due course, the big day arrives, and you will need to report to the show secretary in good time, and suitably attired. Punctuality is essential when judging; to be late is discourteous, and it is extremely inconvenient to the society whose show must run to the clock. You will also feel more comfortable if you have time for a cup of coffee and a 'settling the butterflies' relaxation period before you begin judging. A judge should be smartly turned out, but not mistaken for a chief guest at a smart wedding! Ladies should not wear anything dangly or floaty, and above all you should wear comfortable shoes. Always take wet weather clothing, even if it sounds like an indoor venue; sometimes the large breeds are outside, so go prepared.

It is better to avoid coming face to face with any of your exhibitors prior to judging. This is for no other reason than to stave off any embarrassment that could be caused. You will be introduced to your stewards, and, armed with judging book, pen and judge's rosette, you will make your way to the ring allotted. There is very little space in a standard judging book for any notes you wish to take for the very important critique, so take an extra notebook with you.

If it is your first appointment, you are bound to be feeling a little nervous. If not, you may be over-confident! Even the most experienced Championship show judges read and re-read the Breed Standard each time they judge, and many feel a trace of nerves knowing that all eyes will be on them. The judge will be judging the dogs to the very best of their ability. Everyone will be judging the judge!

You will decide and instruct your stewards on ring procedure, where you wish both the new and the seen dogs to stand; how you will move the dogs, and where the best place is for the line-ups. Remember that the other exhibitors will be interested in the dogs, so try to give the spectators as good a view as possible. As the steward is handing out the ring numbers, take the chance to observe the dogs entering the ring – it can be very revealing. A good steward is invaluable; most work on a voluntary basis, and therefore deserve to be treated with the utmost courtesy. In fact, this is true with regard to all the exhibitors, and certainly all the dogs.

Hopefully, the judge of the day has, as part of his apprenticeship, spent some time as a steward, as much is learnt from that position, watching experienced judges at work. At the start of each class it is important to mark the absentees in the judging book.

International all-round judge Christopher Habig, judging in Sweden, found Ch. Grand Fawns Hagbard to his liking. I was equally impressed by this strong, typical male and gave him Best in Show at the Swedish Great Dane Club Show.

GOING OVER THE DANE

The judge will now view the class as a whole, walking down the line for a quick overall impression of each dog. The dogs are then usually moved around the ring and the general outline and balance of the dog is noted, whether the movement is ground-covering or stilted. Each dog is then examined in turn, the handler helping the dog to adopt their best stance. The judge should stand well back from the dog, as it is impossible to assess overall balance if you are 'on top' of the Dane when the outline is viewed. The judge moves closer to observe rear stance, hock and feet placement and forehand placement, to assess whether the Dane is true in front, to check the proportion of height to length, and to evaluate the flow of neck and topline.

A judge establishes a definite order of going over a dog. There should not be an excessive laying on of hands and body massage. Over-handling by the judge is quite unnecessary in a smooth-coated breed. Individual examination begins at the head, observing width, length and planes from front and sides, noting eye placement, size and colour, the stop; ear placement and size, nostrils and, of course, teeth. Some judges prefer the handler to show them the teeth, rather than risk spread of possible infection going from mouth to mouth.

The judge will then assess the crested neck and shoulder placement, and the whole front assembly. The body will then be evaluated, checking ribs and loin, hindquarters, taking in total rear construction, including testicles in males, and, of course, coat and colour. It is then necessary to see the Dane move. Size and shape of the ring will determine whether the great British triangle is to be favoured – showing the dog going down, across in profile and back to the judge. If the floor is slippery, a mat is provided that permits only up and down movement, and the judge will need to move to the side to assess profile movement.

Calling the memorised Breed Standard to mind will remind you of the desired movement in a Great Dane. Sometimes a dog will move erratically or even pace, and the judge will give another opportunity for correct movement to be shown. General condition of the dog, good coat, well muscled up, bright alert appearance will be taken into account. Type and conformation are, however, the most important considerations.

Make a final tour of the ring to decide on placings. Be decisive, standing and gazing achieves little and only gives the impression that you cannot make up your mind. Ringsiders become bored with slow judging, and handlers become irritated as it is extremely difficult to keep a dog in a show pose for long period of time.

In very large classes it may be necessary to 'short list', and to take another look at the selected few. Whenever possible, place the dogs definitely in the desired order from left to right with a clear "Madam" or "Sir", and positive instructions of the placements. Always give instructions politely; a judge too full of their own importance is a pain in the neck! The only judge more deserving of contempt is the one who is heavy-handed and rough with the dogs.

Mark your judging book, and make brief notes on your winners so that you can more easily call them to mind when writing your critique for the dog papers. Some judges find tape-recorders a positive boon. However, they can malfunction, and since I am so strongly of the opinion that a responsible and sensible critique should follow all judging appointments, I dare not trust my 'memory joggers' to a machine! At the completion of judging the classes, the Best of Breed is awarded to the best Great Dane according to the Breed Standard – not to the Dane that the judge may feel has most chance in the big ring.

HONESTY AND INTEGRITY

Judging is not a PR exercise; it not a popularity contest, nor a way of settling of old scores. It should never be a way of ingratiating yourself, and never a platform to be used for any other reason than putting up the best dogs in your honest opinion, regardless of how much or little winning they have done in the past, and without any consideration of who owns them, who has bred them, and what bloodlines they carry. No matter how impressive a judge's knowledge and experience, if they lack integrity when standing in the middle of the ring then their opinions are of little value.

A judge who is honest and fearless and has integrity can and will improve with experience in the judging ring. Judges of this calibre will go on learning about their chosen breed because they *want* to be good judges. A judge who is dishonest, who can be intimidated, or who lacks integrity, is better forgotten. Showing under such a judge is, frankly, a waste of time, as a win has no worth if it is given for the wrong reasons.

CRITIQUES

You will have collected a catalogue from the secretary on the completion of judging. After thanking your stewards and taking your leave of the secretary and society on completion of any paperwork, go home and get on with your critique whilst everything is fresh in your mind. In an ideal critique, a word picture is given of each dog, plus the reasons why one dog was considered better than another. We must accept that some people have more of a 'way with words' than others, just as some are better handlers than others. Honesty comes to the fore once more. Say what you think and what you saw – without spite, and trying not to be too tactless.

A judging appointment does not make you the world expert on the breed, so do not play 'God for the day'; have some self-control. Your written report should tell about the dogs entered under you on that day. Actually, it will reveal a lot about your knowledge of the breed. Senior, knowledgeable, and, therefore, influential people in the breed will read your critique; they will have seen and probably judged the dogs you are writing about. You will earn their interest, perhaps respect, or even ridicule or dismissal, as a judge of the breed.

YOUR FUTURE AS A JUDGE

It is important to keep records of all judging appointments, including judging book and catalogue, as all this information will be needed if you progress to judge at Championship show level. In this day and age, advice is rarely sought and even less frequently taken. Nevertheless, I would feel I was shirking my own responsibilities to the breed if I did not caution you, on the subject of judging, to make haste slowly!

Always bear in mind that the judge's responsibility is not just to him or herself, not just to the exhibitor and the Danes they show – but to the breed. I make no apologies for repeating: judging your breed is a great responsibility, never to be undertaken lightly!

Chapter Six

ESTABLISHING A LINE

There is a vast difference between someone who breeds Great Danes, and someone who has litters with their Great Dane bitch. A serious breeder is someone who has developed a line of closely related animals, a family, if you like, who have reproduced themselves, fairly accurately, over the generations. The essence of a line is consistency of type, and you will only achieve consistency of type if you are prepared to breed fairly closely. Rushing off to the nearest Champion, regardless of his pedigree, will guarantee you nothing more than lucky dip. Such a mating may produce a wonderful puppy in a varied litter, but the chances of that puppy breeding-on any consistency of type for you are remote.

The only way you will breed good Great Danes consistently is by breeding to good Great Danes – to use dogs that not only fit the Breed Standard but have pedigrees to match. A line does not come overnight or in one or two generations. A line must be worked at and worked for. Line breeding is a means to an end; it is exploiting the past to invest in the future. If there is a secret to line breeding, it is to capitalize on the inherent virtues of a pedigree by doubling up on them and emphasising them. Line breed to typical stock, and you will produce typical stock; line breed to rubbish, and you will produce rubbish.

A line is not a kennel; not a prefix. You may admire two Great Danes with the same prefix. However, one may be sired by an American import and one by a Swedish import, and their dams may not be related at all – so do not ever be confused by thinking a prefix means a line – it does not! So we have established that the essence of a line or strain is consistency of recognisable type, achieved by mating together good, sound, typical Danes of common ancestry.

Of course, to line breed successfully you first have to understand your breed and appreciate true Great Dane type. You must make yourself acquainted with genetic and hereditary faults in the breed, and your priority must be to breed Danes which are free from these serious problems. Before embarking on a line breeding programme, you should serve an apprenticeship in the breed. Attend every breed show and study the breed. You will need to know the breeding of every Dane in the show ring, not just the sire and dam, but four and five generations back.

You will need to consult with the senior breeders for information of dogs long since past. This is not easy, as, perhaps, the breeder of the dog in question will tell you he had a

Ch. Dicarl The Lioness of Jafrak and Ch. Dicarl The Heavyweight, bred out of litter sisters and an integral part of the Dicarl line-bred kennel. Credit for this stunning photograph goes to Diane Pearce, who has taken so many good Dane photos over the years.

glorious head and moved like a dream; someone who regularly stood second to him may remember him as unbalanced with a head like a bucket! You will need to persevere and seek many opinions. If eight people out of ten tell you he had light eyes, whilst the other two assure you that his eyes were black as coal, the chances are that there is something in the rumour the eight are spreading.

BEGINNING YOUR LINE

In a perfect world, you would have purchased a beautifully line-bred puppy bitch who easily gained her title, and you mate her back to her superb Champion grandfather. You would thus be beginning your line. However, life is not like that. Even if you had the luck to own a beautifully bred Champion bitch, you would probably find that her grandfather died three weeks before your girl came into season. So, Utopia aside, what you need is a good, sound, well-balanced typical bitch with a good pedigree. A good pedigree does not necessarily mean a line-bred pedigree in this case; it means a pedigree that is free from any serious faults.

You need a sound, honest bitch to start any sort of breeding. It is important that your first bitch is as good as possible, as there is a probable danger that the first Dane you own tends to become, in your eyes, a model for the future. Perhaps the best advice is not to start your breeding programme with that much-loved bitch just because she is there, but to buy a bitch or two of good conformation, correct type and excellent temperament. A study of your bitch's pedigree will show where the good influences lie, and it is to those you will line-breed.

POTENTIAL DISASTERS

Some years ago, a well-meaning lady brought a Great Dane bitch for me to see. She wanted my advice as to a stud dog and came armed with the pedigree; she was convinced she had line-breeding taped! She announced with great satisfaction that a certain dog appeared six times in her bitch's pedigree and then confided that she had located a dog which boasted the same ancestor as double-grandsire.

I felt impelled to cut short her euphoria by asking if she had actually seen this dog. Of course, she had not. He had died two years before she acquired her first Dane. I knew the dog well, and I had seen him hobbling up and down the ring many times. I had frequently discussed with other senior breeders, which were worse, his hindquarters or his shoulders; we invariably concluded that both those failings were somewhat overshadowed by his appalling head! What looked like a golden opportunity for line breeding was in fact a recipe for disaster.

Further study of the pedigree showed that in the fifth generation a bitch appeared twice. She was not a Champion, but she was a good, sound, typical, well-balanced Great Dane. Elsewhere in the pedigree there was another dog with similar virtues. They bore quite different prefixes, yet they were litter brother and sister. Here was something on which to build. We discussed available stud dogs. I knew of a good dog who was out of a bitch sired by yet another litter brother. By using that dog, the well-meaning novice had placed her foot on the ladder of a line-breeding programme.

Who could fail to be impressed by this line of Swedish Great Danes? Bred to type, a sight to gladden any breeder's heart. Dane enthusiasts worldwide know and respect doyen of the breed, Ulla Magnusson. Her husband, Curt, is pictured on the right.

She will need to give each successive generation equal consideration: to dilute faults in order to consolidate virtues. By the time she gets to her fifth generation of homebred stock, she may be able to claim that she has 'a line'.

IN-BREEDING

In-breeding is an intensified form of line-breeding and is, without doubt, best left to the experts. If there are skeletons in the closet you can guarantee that an incestuous mating will bring them rattling to the surface. The less experienced breeder should be aware that line-breeding demands equally high standards as in-breeding: it is a modification that will produce the same results but less dangerously.

OUT-CROSSING

This is not a particular system of breeding. It can only be useful as an event in a line-breeding programme, to introduce some 'new' point, not to eliminate an existing one. While an outcross mating may bring a certain virtue you seek, it will also bring faults which you maybe did not have before, and which may take considerable breeding out. In out-crossing it is essential that a return to the original line should be made immediately after the cross.

POINTS TO REMEMBER

1. Like begets like, and the mating of opposites does not produce the happy medium. Two wrongs do not make a right. A weak-headed, snipy-muzzled bitch mated to a dog with an overdone, coarse, heavy head, will not produce correct heads.

2. Be honest with yourself about your bitch's failings and use a dog who is absolutely correct in that department.

3. Never ever double up on a fault.

4. Remember that the title of Champion does not confer extra breeding value on any dog. His progeny alone can do this.

5. It is useless to line-breed to mediocre animals. It is possible to inherit faults not necessarily displayed in the parents. Each puppy receives twenty-five per cent of its inheritance from grandparents.

6. Always welcome advice from those qualified to give it. Beware of opinions of the spiteful or the biased.

7. Be aware that silk purses are rarely made from sows' ears.

8. Aim to establish a line and found a strain that is a credit both to your name and prefix and to your chosen breed.

9. Never ever forget the element of luck. For no matter how genuine or dedicated you are, without that precious magic element, success as a breeder can be heartbreakingly elusive. I am well aware of how lucky I was in establishing the Dicarl line.

Chapter Seven

BREEDING GREAT DANES

If you have decided to share your life with a Great Dane bitch, the time may come when you think of having a litter with her. Please think and think again before you embark on such an undertaking. Do not underestimate the hard work, and the possible expense, should things not go absolutely smoothly. You may have problems finding suitable homes, and then be faced with growing pups eating you out of house and home, and the on-going responsibility for the Danes you have brought into the world.

Your responsibility does not end as your puppies leave for their new homes. The new owner may find that the appealing babe has grown into a wilful teenager with which they cannot cope. That sizeable delinquent, with an equally sizeable appetite, is your responsibility. Do you have the facilities to take back and rehouse any of your puppies which become unwanted? Dane rescue services are already over-worked. If you are simply looking for another Dane pup to enrich your family, it may be wiser to buy one from a reputable breeder and avoid all the hard work and worry?

Should you be under the misapprehension that you are breeding for 'the good of the bitch', let me assure you that this is utter nonsense. It does not harm a bitch to not have a litter in her lifetime.

BREEDING STOCK

If after much thought and soul-searching, you decide it is your serious intention to breed with your bitch, you *must* be sure that, much as you love her, she is of sufficient merit and quality to breed with. She must be sound in body and mind, she must be typical of the breed with no outstanding faults, and she must be free from hereditary defects.

You will need to look at your bitch objectively, as we know there is no such thing as a perfect specimen, so you must evaluate just where your bitch scores and fails. The stud dog should be chosen to complement her best features, and, hopefully, to improve on her less good features.

RESPONSIBILITIES

ETHICAL: Your responsibility is not only to your bitch but also to the breed. With your litter you must aim to improve upon or at least maintain the best features of the breed as demanded by the Breed Standard. Remember that your puppies, in turn, may be bred from. By breeding a litter you are taking an active part in the future of the breed.

FINANCIAL: Having a litter can be a very expensive business. You will need to think about where the whelping will take place, and what equipment you require. It may be necessary to make or purchase a whelping box; you will need a heat lamp and bedding materials. The stud fee and travelling expenses must be taken into account, as well as possibly time off work to supervise the mating, whelping, and the rearing of the puppies.

Veterinary costs can mount alarmingly. Bitches often whelp during the night, which can mean an expensive out-of-hours visit. Whelping complications may arise; a caesarian is a major financial outlay. Weaning and rearing costs can be frightening with a giant breed, especially if puppy sales are slow and some of the babies are still with you at ten to twelve weeks.

TO MOTHER AND BABIES: You may think it is unnecessary to be warned of the responsibility towards your bitch and her puppies. Obviously you love your bitch very much, and you will be equally caring about her babies. However, love is not always enough, and sometimes it is too much. There is a difference between sentiment and responsibility.

It is a fact that Great Danes can whelp extremely large litters, twelve or fourteen whelps are not unusual. A Great Dane bitch is happy, contented, and unflustered if she has six or eight babies to care for. It is better to have that number beautifully reared, rather than a dozen less well reared who will not develop their full potential of bone, a fault which will be passed down to their own litters in due course. Finding six wonderful new homes is certainly more feasible than finding twelve at the same time. Firm bookings have a way of evaporating when puppies are actually available.

Puppies can be culled on the first day by a veterinary surgeon; there is no distress to the dam, she is simply taken out to spend a penny and returns and settles with her 'copeable' litter.

PLANNING A LITTER
Decision made, now comes, with just ordinary luck, one of the most joyful and exhausting times of your life. Good luck and on we go!

It is better to breed from your bitch between the ages of two and three and a half. Before then she will not be fully mature, and after four years the likelihood of problems may increase. At the time of mating, your Dane should be in firm, fit condition; breeding from an overweight bitch invites complications. It may well be advisable or even courteous to discuss your bitch's future litter with her breeder. Valuable information may be passed on and you may find it comforting to have an experienced breeder to turn to in times of anxiety.

If you do not already have a good and trusting relationship with your vet, now is the time to introduce yourself and your mother-to-be, as the vet's services will be needed to some degree. During the visit, collect same worming tablets for use on your bitch a few weeks before her season is due, and check that vaccinations are up to date.

Is your bitch good enough to breed from? This Dane has excellent conformation and true breed type. She also has appalling front feet, showing that all animals have faults as well as virtues. Without doubling up on the feet fault, she was line-bred to Ch. The Weightlifter, and her daughter became Wyn Doyle's lovely Ch. Dicarl The Dreamseller – who, incidentally had correct feet!

The stud dog must be chosen wisely on his own merits and those on his pedigree. Successful in the show ring and as a sire, Ch. Yacanto Top Gun is a dog of great masculinity, strength and substance.

Diane Pearce.

Do not be in too much of a hurry to decide upon the stud dog, and take everything into account – apart from geographical convenience and your personal feelings about the owner of the male! When you have reached the momentous decision, contact the owner to establish whether your bitch is acceptable to his or her dog. The owner of the chosen dog may have doubts about the wisdom of the mating; that is their prerogative.

Assuming all is well, the stud fee should be agreed in advance of the mating. It is advisable to pay the stud fee. To agree to a 'puppy back' or 'pick of litter' arrangement can cause misunderstandings and bad feelings at collection time. It is always courteous to invite the owner of the stud dog to see your litter and to view favourably his or her possible desire to purchase one of the puppies.

You should be aware that the stud fee is for the services of the dog; it is not dependent on the arrival of a healthy litter. Should the bitch fail to conceive or rear her puppies, a free stud may be offered, by a reasonable and sympathetic stud dog owner.

THE MATING

At the first signs of the bitch coming into season, the stud dog owner should be notified. The exact day of mating cannot be arranged, but it is likely be from twelve to fourteen days hence. Every breeder has their own method of telling when the bitch is ready to accept the stud dog. Generally, when the swelling around the vulva begins to decrease and when the colour changes from bright red to transparent pink, the time is nigh. If, when meeting another dog, she cocks her tail over to the side, or the owner tickling at the base of her tail brings the same reaction, then she is ready.

In their anxiety to effect a successful mating, most owners take their bitches to the stud dog far too early. Matings taking place on the wrong day is the reason for more bitches missing than any other single cause. An experienced stud dog knows when a bitch is right, and he may not oblige until then. It is possible for your vet to give ovulation tests to ensure the correct time.

Two services, spaced a couple of days apart are often suggested. Sperm can live for about four days in a bitch, and it is not until she ovulates that fertilisation takes place. Sometimes there is worry or confusion about the due date of the whelping. The gestation period is nine weeks from the day of fertilisation, which is not necessarily the day of mating. Do not panic if your bitch is late – or early for that matter; I have known normal whelpings from between 57 and 68 days. In a text-book mating, the Danes will flirt and play a little, always on leads and under control. When the male begins to get serious, it is the responsibility of the owner of the bitch to hold her steady and still until and during the tie. The tie occurs when the muscles of the vagina constrict and hold the swollen penis in place. It is the penetration and ejaculation that ensures the litter, the tie is not actually necessary, but it is usual in Great Danes, and usually lasts for about twenty minutes. During the tie, it is common for the male to turn so he is standing rear to rear with the bitch.

Obviously, the whole business of breeding a litter from mating to whelping is a specialised business, and there are a number of books which deal exclusively with this subject. All novice breeders would be well advised to read as much as possible in order to be as fully prepared as possible.

THE IN-WHELP BITCH

For the first weeks following mating, the bitch should follow her normal routine of feeding and exercise. You may detect slight changes in her manner: she may become more affectionate, 'clingy'; she may go off her food at around three weeks; some think a watery or creamy discharge a good sign. Eventually you will see a thickening of the loins and a pinkish enlarged look to the nipples. Victor Harrild of the Moonsfield Great Danes had his own method of charting pregnancy. He would measure the bitch's waist at time of mating, and from three weeks onwards. At the five week stage, he could make an accurate prediction – I never remember Victor and his tape measure being wrong!

Your veterinary surgeon can feel for whelps at a crucial stage, and modern technology provides ultrasonic scan equipment that can actually tell how many whelps are in the uterus. We never went in for any of this. We waited, hoped, and relied upon our knowledge of our bitches. If, at about five weeks, you think a litter is due, then increase your Dane's food. She needs 'good' food. Eggs, cheese, fish, milk and sensible additions of added vitamins and sterilised bone meal.

Prepare the whelping area in good time and introduce your bitch to it a couple of weeks before the happy event. You will need a wooden box that is large enough for a Dane to lie out fully stretched. A rail should be fitted all the way around the inside, a couple of inches from the floor. This gives the puppies a safety area should the bitch flop down heavily, trapping a babe against the sides. Great Danes make good mothers, generally, and do not mean to be clumsy, but the very size and weight and perhaps tiredness of the bitch, can result in accidents. The whelping box must be situated somewhere quiet and totally free from draughts and I would suggest your bitch should be sleeping in the bed about a week before the due date. I recommend a heat lamp be suspended over the bed; in a heatwave it can always be turned off, but it is a fact that more puppies die of cold than lack of food.

THE WAITING GAME

Dane bitches carry their babies in different ways. By eight weeks she may look like an old goat! Your elegant, beautiful bitch may have a tummy almost touching the ground and a sagging bony topline. Do not worry, she will get her figure back and be back in the show ring, if that is your desire. All of the Champion bitches that lived with me had a litter before gaining their title, and Tarbaby won a CC after four litters – so do not be distressed if she looks awful!

In contrast, your bitch could be carrying her babies well up 'in the ribs', and you may be doubtful she is actually in whelp. I have known eight bouncing babes born to a bitch who hardly showed a sign of pregnancy. Most Dane bitches are more loving and more dependent upon their owners in the last stages of pregnancy. She will like you to admire and stroke her tummy; and the thrill of feeling and seeing a 'bump' that is one of the precious babies, is something very special.

THE WHELPING

The whelping box should be lined with newspaper. Danes just love to tear up a newspaper bed and make a nest for the whelping. This furious activity will go on for hours, even days, before whelping commences. The bitch may go off her food at this stage; then again she may not. Her temperature will drop to around 98 degrees fahrenheit before whelping. She will be restless, with a faraway look in her eyes, panting heavily, and licking at her nether regions.

In readiness for the whelping, you will need:

Warm water and disinfectant (to keep your hands clean).
Clean, rough towels (some pups may need a brisk rubbing).
A pair of blunt scissors (to cut a cord, if necessary).
Extra newspaper (whelping can be messy, and newspaper is very absorbent).
A small cardboard box, plus a covered hot-water bottle (this is for the puppies while Mum is occupied with the delivery of another).
A reference book on whelping.
Your vet's telephone number.

Once your bitch begins to strain, you will see her arching her back, and lifting her tail, and a muscular ripple will pass down the length of her body. The water bag will break; the lovely clean bed will be soaked, and shortly afterwards you will have your first puppy. The bitch will probably clean the puppy herself, freeing it from its sac, biting its cord, and licking furiously.

If she is a maiden bitch and a little confused, you may need to help her. Let her see what you are doing to her baby; gently pull the membrane of the sac away from the pup's nose, cleaning the nostrils. Pinch the umbilical cord firmly, about four inches away from the pup, and cut at that point on the side closest to the dam. Rub the baby dry and praise the bitch, encouraging her to take an interest in the new arrival. You will be amazed at the puppies' natural instinct to head straight to the milk bar and latch on to a teat with a suction that is awe-inspiring. Little paws paddle away, stimulating the release of the first milk containing colostrum. This is all-important, as it contains the mother's antibodies to disease.

This process will be repeated with every new whelp. If your bitch is producing a large litter, she may take a rest in the midst of the whelping. I am never happy with long-drawn-out whelpings. If my bitches went more than a couple of hours between puppies, I would consult my vet. The longer the whelping takes, the more tired the bitch becomes. Never allow your Dane to strain for any length of time without producing a puppy; she may need help – professional help. A good vet would prefer to be called unnecessarily rather than the bitch run into trouble because the owner was not sure.

Each puppy has an afterbirth, although this is not always delivered with the puppy. The bitch will eat these, and this should be allowed as they contain vitamins and nutriment. They also act as a laxative, and if she is not interested in consuming the last few in a large litter, by all means remove them. Some Dane bitches will welcome a cool drink of milk with a couple of egg yolks beaten in, between whelps, others may show little interest in food of any kind for several days.

When the whelping is over, your Dane will stretch out fully and appear totally relaxed. Even if her tummy appears empty, if she is still curled up and not settled, then there may be

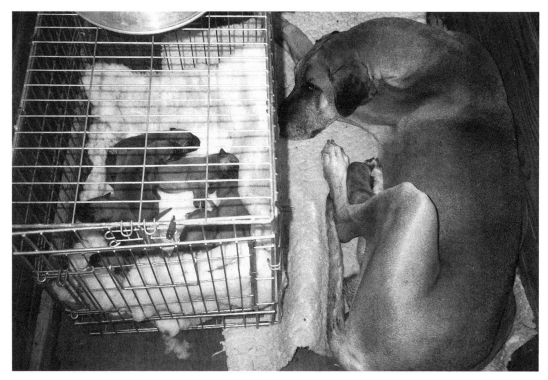

During whelping, the puppies may be put in a warm crate alongside the mother, giving her room to cope with the next arrival without distractions.

It is amazing how instinctively and quickly the newborn puppies find the teat and start to suckle.

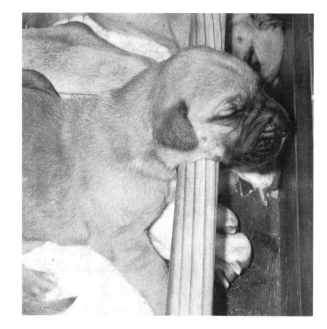

The safety (furrowing) rail is a safeguard to prevent the mother from lying on her puppies.

The whelping box, complete with safety rail, overhead heat-lamp, six sturdy puppies, and a mother who thinks that six pups are plenty to cope with!

another puppy or a retained afterbirth. Either way, ask your vet to check your bitch after whelping. An injection will probably be administered to clean out the uterus, and it is better safe than sorry.

When both you and your vet are happy with mother and babies, put a lead on your bitch and take her out to relieve herself. You will need a lead, as Dane mums are very reluctant to leave their babies for the first few days. Take this opportunity to give her a nice, fresh bed. Newspaper is fine for a few days, and then I recommend the fleecy type of bedding. This is excellent as the pups can get a good grip with their hindfeet as they pummel the milk bar.

After the bitch has been out, allow her to return and settle with her litter. She will organise them to her liking. There will be deep sighs coming from her, and a contented hum from the pups! Check the temperature: remember how important warmth is to newborn puppies. Then you can relax and survey one of the most beautiful sights in the world – a Great Dane proudly nursing her litter. You will have spotted a couple of Champions already. Well, enjoy. The real work is still to come!

REARING THE LITTER

For the first few days you will need to check mother and puppies every hour or so, just to see all is well. Encourage your bitch to take light meals frequently, and *lots* of fluids. Offer her clean fresh water each time you visit. Most Danes are so besotted with their babies that they are loath to leave the whelping box, so offer her sustenance in her bed, placing the bowl between her front legs. If she is reluctant to eat, try placing a little of the food on her front legs. She will 'tidy up', and this may awaken her interest in food. Eventually her appetite will return – indeed, some bitches never lose it. However, I have found more anxiety among novice breeders over loss of appetite post-whelping, than any other problem. A useful tip at any time for a reluctant feeder is to make a sponge cake and offer her this. You just need a plain cake – you do not need jam or cream filling!

Healthy, thriving puppies are fairly quiet; an occasional yelp or grunting and a deal of twitching will be observed. If there is constant noise, mewing or complaining, then check the puppies. They may be too hot or too cold, or hungry, or unwell. If you see any yellowish-coloured diarrhoea, then consult your veterinary surgeon immediately. Keep a close eye on your bitch's undercarriage, and clip the puppies' nails regularly as sharp nails can cause great discomfort to the dam.

DEWCLAWS

Between three and five days, your veterinary surgeon will remove the dewclaws. Not all Great Dane breeders see the necessity for the removal of dewclaws; I do. They are a useless and dangerous appendage, and, in my opinion, ruin the clean lines of a good front. I have never had a puppy suffer any ill effects from the procedure properly done, but I have seen adverse effects and injury on grown Danes *with* dewclaws.

WEANING

At about ten to twelve days, the puppies will begin to open their eyes, and no matter how many litters you have bred, it is always an occasion for comment and excitement. The eyes

Weaning is a messy business – but you can always get the mother in after the puppies have finished eating to clean them up.

The feeding bowl can be raised on bricks to stop the puppies paddling through it – although some puppies will still find a way!

will be blue, and they will darken later on. The pups will begin to pull themselves up on chunky little legs and stagger about like tiny, bleary-eyed prehistoric monsters.

This is the time to begin helping the bitch with the feeding. Sometimes the mother is doing the puppies so well that they resemble fat, contented slugs, and weaning can be a messy and frustrating business.

A nice, evenly-matched litter at three weeks of age.

Great Dane puppies need *the best* of everything. The growth rate is tremendous. Starting from 11/2lb to 2lb at birth, they double body-weight weekly, and to achieve the required strength of bone they need top-quality foods and the addition of bone meal. Size and bone are bred into the puppy and, given correct feeding, full potential will be achieved. Every breeder has their own methods of weaning and rearing. I admit that my ideas are quite old-fashioned, yet I have no argument with more modern, up-to-date techniques.

We began with raw, scraped best beef, a walnut-sized piece held in one hand and a puppy in the other. I defy anyone not to beam at the sight of a fat baby violently tugging and sucking at the first taste of meat. We used a proprietary brand of baby food, made up as directed on the packet, and introduced each pup individually to this delicious 'goo' until eventually the bowl could be put down, and the litter would paddle through, consuming the contents with an appalling lack of table manners!

From one or two small meals a day, the build-up is rapid and by four to five weeks, puppies will be having five meals a day and mother's milk as well. By this time your bitch should have her own special bed, raised, where she can lie and survey her puppies at all times, but they cannot get at her. She will join them in the communal bed at the appropriate times, but she can have a bit of peace when she feels the need.

The expensive time is here, and you should never stint on rearing your Dane babies. If you are feeding meat and biscuit, always give the best, and supplement with eggs, fish, cheese

Young Noah Le Mare of the Helmlake Great Danes: It is fascinating watching the puppies as they grow and as their personalities start to emerge.

etc. Fresh air and preferably sunshine are also needed. In the old days breeders tended to aim for summer litters, appreciating the benefits of "sun on the puppies' backs". Puppies need to play, so safe toys should be available. We found that cardboard boxes gave hours of pleasure, and a raised, wooden platform, only six or nine inches off the ground will appeal to puppies and stop them lying on damp or cold ground. All puppies require worming, and you must follow your vet's instructions on brand and dosage; he/she will also advise on inoculations.

PUPPY WATCHING

A litter of Great Dane puppies is irresistible. Hours will be spent just watching them – from their first cautious teeterings on the brink, to the bold wrecking crew they will become. Individual characters and personalities will emerge, and your time will be taken up by feeding, cleaning, cuddling, chastising and admiring. You will see them change almost daily, developing and improving. Inevitably, at all times there will be a biggest one and a smallest one. Do not put too much store on size of pups. The smallest baby can often end up the largest adult; it is more sensible to admire a pup for breed type than for size or weight.

The stance and demeanour may give clues to the finished product. A puppy that is proud and carries himself or herself well, that struts about with head held high and stands well-balanced with alertness, may have natural attributes for the show ring. The heads of Great

Ch. Dicarl The Crying Time, pictured at four months. To the inexperienced eye, she looks less than promising.

Ch. Dicarl The Crying Time in maturity. This is a wonderful illustration of ugly duckling into swan. At four months, she is long cast, short on the leg, and desperately needing to grow into ears and tail! In maturity she was quite beautiful.

Dane pups require great scrutiny, and a poor head, be it wedge-shaped, snipey, lacking muzzle-width and depth, will be noticeable against a good head of strength, with balance of skull and foreface, and even a slight Roman nose. Eye colour can change and darken way past the puppy playpen stage. Unfortunately, this is also true of mouths, and a breeder cannot be sure of a correct mouth until way past the baby teeth age.

Strong bone is apparent, and tight, cat feet are wonderful, but feet can go through horrendous stages. The Contender, for example, had enormous, flat feet at twelve weeks. They could only be compared to rhubarb leaves at the base of his tree-trunk-like legs. I feel compelled to point out that his feet improved enough for him to win 19 CCs and the Working Group at Crufts!

Tail sets can cause confusion, and I have, truthfully, never seen a puppy with a low-set tail. Low croups develop, alas, later in life. Dane pups do tend to look a little long cast; however, the distance between the last rib and the pelvis should be short. Basic conformation should be studied and knowledge of the development of the puppies' ancestors can be very helpful.

It has to be said that the most promising puppy can disappoint, and some of the best Great Danes ever bred end up in pet homes as their show ring potential was overlooked. I have seen puppies of eight weeks in other breeders' kennels that I would have died for, only to see them in maturity in the show ring and to be greatly relieved that I had kept my cheque book in my handbag when I coveted them in the nest. Others I wouldn't have given two beans for as babies, have made quality adults to whom I have given top honours in the ring.

My general rule was that if I liked a puppy at birth, and still liked it at about six weeks, then that pup stayed until six months of age. I ignored all the ugly duckling stages in between: the ten-to-two fronts, high back-ends, gangling or dumpy bodies, ears flying, the 'I can't be touched by a judge' stage, were all taken on board. If any Dane pup stayed with me past six months, they stayed for life. I was always more wary of pups that looked 'too good, too soon'. Early maturers tend to go past their best too soon, and I, personally, prefer puppies that are slow maturers.

Tendellie, who was the top-winning Dane at one time, and another Crufts Group Winner, did not win a thing in Puppy Classes. But, to be fair, and also to confuse things further, The Weightlifter was unbeatable as a Puppy and was a Champion by thirteen months of age. He then went through a rangy stage, rendering him unsuitable for the show ring. It was many months before he was ready for any more CCs.

Enjoy your puppy watching, and although you will be sad when the pups finally leave home, you will have the joy every Christmas when cards arrive with photographs inside of your babies, grown into adored, adult Great Danes.

Chapter Eight

THE GREAT DANE IN BRITAIN

EARLY YEARS IN THE SHOW RING

Initially, the breed was known as the Boarhound and was regarded as a Sporting dog. However, at the Crystal Palace show in 1875 there were Danes in the prize list in both the extra class for Foreign Sporting dogs and the extra class for foreign dogs not used in Field Sports! The breed was also referred to as the Ulmer Hound, Ulmer Mastiff, Danish and Royal German Hunting Hound. Looking through the earliest volumes of the Stud Book, we find that many of the dogs entered in the Foreign dog classes are not identified by breed. The first Boarhound to be identified as such, and to win a prize at a dog show, was Captain Palmer MP's 'Sam'. We have no other information about this dog, apart from the owner's name, except that the dog was second in the extra class at the show held at the Agricultural Hall, Islington in June 1862. He was then placed third in the class for Large Foreign dogs at the Ashburnham Hall Show in London in 1863. The Islington Show was reported in the *Illustrated London News*, with an illustration of Sam by Harrison Weir. It is noted that Sam was the largest dog at the show, and that there were a total of fifty-four dogs entered in the class. The other successful Boarhound of the time was Mr Hemming's 'Nero' – the winner in both Foreign Sporting and Non-sporting Classes.

The first breed classes were held at the Alexandra Palace Show, which was run by the Kennel Club in January 1879. The judge was Mr Edgar Hanbury. The first prize winner in the Boarhound or Great Dane class was Mr Adcock's 'Prosperina', who was a blue-brindle in colour, born in 1876 and had been imported, though we do not know from where. The second Boarhound class was at the Kennel Club's own show, held in Brighton in November 1879. Mr Honey's 'Marco' was the first prize winner, and as he had been second at Alexandra Palace, he was the top-winning Boarhound of that year. The judge at Brighton was Mr Lort, who was more closely involved with Gundogs.

In 1880 there were three shows with classes for the breed, and for the first time we see entries made by one of the foremost German breeders, Herr Messter, who lived just outside Berlin. His 'Katzie' was third at Crystal Palace; 'Marco III' was second at the same show, and Mr Thomson's home-bred 'Juno', was second at Alexandra Palace. The only dog to win at more than one show was Mr Petrzywalski's 'Sultan II' with a second place at Alexandra Palace and third place at Crystal Palace.

THE FIRST CHAMPION

In the 1882 Stud Book, which contains the show results for 1881, the Boarhound has its own section for the first time. This is equivalent to the breed receiving Championship status, for at this time Challenge Certificates did not exist, and a dog won its title by winning four first prizes – three in ordinary classes and the fourth in the special class called the Champion Class. The first Great Dane to do this and so become the first Champion in the breed was Mr Petrzywalski's Ch. Sultan II. His wins were first at Alexandra Palace in June 1882, Crystal Palace in January 1883, Crystal Palace in July 1883, and Henley in October 1883, winning his title with first placing in the Champion Class at the Crystal Palace Show in January 1884. This was an important year for the breed, as its name was changed from Boarhound to Great Dane in the Stud Book.

Sultan II was described by Dr Gordon Stables, a prolific writer on dogs, as "a large brindle pure Boarhound, or more correctly called Great Dane; about 35 inches at shoulder, weighs in fair condition, not fat, 12 stone or 168 lbs; is very active, good tempered, and very faithful and intelligent. He is by Sultan I, out of Leo, this last having won several gold and silver medals abroad." In total, he won four ordinary first prizes and five firsts in the Champion Class. The second Great Dane Champion was the fawn Ch. Cedric The Saxon from Herr Messter's kennel, though owned by Mr R.L.Pemberton. The basis of this kennel was Nero I, and all the extended pedigrees of this time go back to the mating of Nero I with Else.

Herr Messter started his kennel in 1873, and Jean Lanning mentions "his greatest triumphs were in the years between 1880 and 1890, and from the records it appears that he took the breed and the shows by storm. In Berlin in 1880 he had thirty-two Great Danes entered, and in 1881, 1883 and 1885 he exhibited in London, on each occasion showing twenty dogs. When in Russia at the St Petersburg Show in 1887, he exhibited twenty-two Great Danes."

LEADING SHOW DOGS

By the time that Ch. Cedric The Saxon was being shown, the rules for gaining the title of Champion had been altered; there had been an increase in the number of dog shows so it was becoming too easy to win the four first prizes. The class that had been called the Champion Class was now known as the Challenge Class, and the qualifying wins were seven first prizes with three in the Challenge Class. To make sure that the title holder was really worthy of this honour, one of the Challenge Class wins had to be at the Kennel Club's own show, or Birmingham National. Cedric won his title at Weymouth Show in July 1885, having won the Challenge Class at the Kennel Club's own show held at the Crystal Palace a few days before.

He was also the winner of the Challenge Class at the first specialist show held for Great Danes, in June 1885 in the grounds of the Ranelagh Club and organised by the Great Dane Club, formed two years earlier. Jean Lanning reports that Gambier Bolton was the judge (he drew up the first Standard for the breed) and that "this was just the time when the breed was reaching the height of its popularity here, and the sixty dogs made a wonderful show, benched under the lime trees in these historic grounds. Never before had such a gathering of these magnificent dogs been seen in this country, among them the great fawn dog Cedric The Saxon, perfect in symmetry. With Captain Graham, the noted Irish Wolfhound

King Edward V11 and Queen Alexandra regularly visited the show benches.

Illustration from Britain's King & Queen by Thomas Paul, 1902.

authority, Rawdon Lee carefully measured Cedric, who stood 331/4 inches at the shoulder. The two experts then took the height of several of the biggest animals present, and found 'it was extraordinary how 35 inch and 36 inch animals dwindled down, some of them nearly half an inch at a time'! Other tall dogs exhibited at Ranelagh were Herbert Leal who stood 333/4 inches at the shoulders and weighed 182lbs and Mr Riego's brindle dog Cid Campeador, who stood exactly 331/2 inches and weighed 175lbs."

Cid Campeador was an imported dog who became the third Champion in the breed. This meant that the first bitch Champion was actually the fourth Champion to be made up. She was the German-bred Vendetta, who won her qualifying prize at the Kennel Club's own show held at Barn Elms in June 1887. She was one of the top-winning Great Danes of the 19th century, with fourteen firsts in the Challenge Class, as well as five ordinary first prizes. Vendetta was by Dr Castor's Harras out of Ramsberger Flora, bred by Herr Ramsberger and owned by Mr E.G.Martin.

In 1888 the rules for the title Champion altered once again. Shows were divided into one and two point shows, based on the number of entries. Wins in the Challenge Class at a one point show counted one point to a title, and there were six points needed, with two points gained at Birmingham or the Kennel Club's own shows. The first British-bred Champion was Mr Sawtell's Ch. Ivanhoe, who was a son of Ch. Cedric The Saxon out of the German-bred Ch. Challymead Queen. Ivanhoe was also the winner of the Challenge class at the first Crufts Show in 1891.

Breeders of other 'giant' breeds also took an interest in the Great Dane. Mr Hood Wright, who was more famous for his Deerhounds, owned Ch. Selwood Sambo and Ch. Selwood Ninon, both bred by Mr Alberti. Mr Hood Wright was also at one time the Secretary of the Great Dane Club. Sambo was the first Great Dane to win his title under the current Challenge Certificate system, winning his title at Nottingham Champion Show in 1896. He traced back to Herr Messter's breeding. In the Stud Book his grandsire is given as Morcan, but in Dr Morrell Mackenzie's book, it is Moreau, and with the passage of time it is impossible to say which is the correct pedigree. Sambo was the sire of one Champion – Mr Pendry's Ch. Mammoth Queen. Mr Coop owned the Windle kennel that was also famous for its Borzois, and for his Ch. Windle Princess, out of Fatima, who was a double-granddaughter of Ch. Sultan II, the very first Champion.

THE REDGRAVE KENNEL

The next important event in Great Dane history was in 1896 when Violet Horsfall imported two Danes from Germany – Emma II, who was renamed Emma of Redgrave and who was in-whelp to Mr Dobbelmann's Dutch Champion, Bosto Colonia, and her son from a previous litter, Hannibal of Redgrave. Hannibal became a Champion in February 1897 and was described as "though not very big, he was a beautifully built dog, showing power and grace in every line". Emma was "a splendidly made bitch" but "the most striking point about these grand hounds was their look of 'race' or breeding, so often missing in present-day Danes. Ch. Hannibal had the true Dane eye, dark, fierce and dominating, and in the head of Ch. Emma can be seen the same look of reserve power." This was written by E. Mackay Scott in 1908.

Emma gained her title at Birmingham in November 1898, and one of the puppies from her litter became Ch. Valentine of Redgrave – the litter was born on Valentine's Day 1897. Valentine herself was the dam of six Champions. The Great Danes from the Redgrave kennel traced back to Herr Messter's breeding, and to the breeding of Herr Ulrich from Southern Germany, who had Herr Messter's breeding behind his dogs as well. Seventeen Great Dane Champions were made up before the turn of the century, and Mrs Horsfall dominated the show ring until 1906 when at the peak of her kennel's fame she stopped exhibiting. She still retained an interest in the breed, writing to the dog papers at intervals on the state of the breed, and she continued to judge.

Ch. Valentine of Redgrave, and the other two Champions of 1900 were Valentine's son, Ch. Viceroy of Redgrave, and Ch. Vanda of Redgrave. Both these were by Ch. Hannibal of Redgrave. Vanda's dam was Ch. Selwood Ninon, who Violet Horsfall must have bought from Mr Hood Wright. Viceroy was considered the best Great Dane up to that time and was

Ch. Viceroy of Redgrave: This dog finished his show career with twenty-one CCs to his credit.

described by Mrs Horsfall as "a golden brindle dog, weighs 147lbs in hard condition, and scales 33¾ inches at the shoulder. He is a big dog that at once strikes one as being very active and having splendid galloping powers. His limbs are enormous and the bone of his fore legs is extraordinary and carried right down below the fore knee, and at the same time as straight as a terrier's. He has the kind of head that could never grow coarse or 'cheeky', his skull being so fine and his foreface of such tremendous depth and squareness and so well filled in below the eyes.

"He never carries his tail too high, even when excited. His ears are carried as in the illustration, and his eyes are a dark, tawny yellow, matching the brightest brindle of his coat, which is sleek and glossy. Give him the neck and carriage of Ch. Thor of Redgrave and he would be absolute perfection. His neck is not a bad shape, but he does not arch it in the grand fashion of Thor. He has never been beaten, has won twelve Championships and eighty-four first and special prizes at the only twelve shows at which he has been exhibited, and the thirty-guinea challenge plate for the best non-sporting dog in the whole show at the Crystal Palace."

Viceroy finished his career with twenty-one CCs, overtaking his sire's total of sixteen, but only keeping the breed record until 1913. The success of the Redgraves was based on Ch. Valentine, who was the dam of six Champions, one of them being Viceroy. Mrs Horsfall also imported the cropped harlequin dog, Lord Ronald of Redgrave, and the bitch, Lot of Redgrave, also a harlequin. Mating these together gave Mrs Sparks' foundation bitch, Lass of Redgrave, who was mated to the brindle Ch. Viceroy of Redgrave to give two harlequin Champions in Ch. Superba and Ch. Loris of Stapleton.

Lord Ronald was the leading harlequin of his day and was described as "a beautifully marked harlequin dog, he stands 32 inches high and weighs 140lbs. His cropped ears will at once attract attention in the illustration, and afford a picture of what the Great Dane could be made to look like without the anti-cropping edict. His eyes are dark brown, his tail carried perfectly and his neck is fit for a sculptor's model. He is noted for his Great Dane 'character', standing straight up, looking as if he would go for anybody and anything. He has plenty of bone, and great muscular development, and is wonderfully active, and the only failing his owner regrets is that he is not two inches higher at the shoulder."

CH. CONN OF CLEVEYS

Once Mrs Horsfall stopped exhibiting, the top winning dog was Mr Kirman's Ch. Conn of Cleveys, who broke the breed record to end up with a total of twenty-seven CCs. He was by Ch. Tiger of Cleethorpes, a grandson of Ch. Viking of Redgrave, out of Ch. Valentine of Highfield, a daughter of Ch. Thor of Redgrave. Dr Morrell Mackenzie described him as "probably the most perfectly coloured fawn that has ever been seen. He gained his first Championship when just twelve months old at the Birkenhead Show, under the continental judge, Herr Esser. He described him as 'a wonderful dog in fine condition, colour and coat', also remarking that 'if such animals were bred the breed would soon show great progress'. Conn has certainly fulfilled his youthful promise and there is no dog that is more sought after in the whole of England, while he is one of the few Great Danes that have been successful in variety classes."

CH. MISS AILEEN

The outstanding brood bitch in the decade up to the First World War was Dr and Mrs Osburne's Ch. Miss Aileen, a daughter of Ch. Viceroy. She was the dam of four Lindville Champions, from three litters by the Ch. Thor of Redgrave son, Ch. Boy Bob. Dr Morrell Mackenzie wrote: "Ch. Boy Bob requires no adjective as a prefix. He has, I believe, at one time or another beaten every dog in England of his breed that has any claims to fame. It is, however, not only on the bench that he is famous as there is no dog to compare with him as a sire; father of two Champions he has other children who are making names for themselves every day and at every show. Once an inmate of Violet Horsfall's famous kennel, he now belongs to Alfred Walker of Lytham."

When this was written, Ch. Fergus and Ch. Thunderer of Lindville were the only ones of this breeding to have been made up, and the Doctor considered "Thunderer, like Fergus, has a wonderfully long head, with deep square muzzle, combined with a short body, deep brisket and the soundest of legs, which is a sine qua non for any aspirant to show honours that comes from these kennels." He also wrote of Miss Aileen: "It must not be thought, however, that her matronly services are superior to her show qualities, for she is built on the most graceful lines, with excellent body and legs, topped by a long slender neck and splendid head."

COLOUR BREEDING

The first blue Champion to be made up was Miss Dickinson's Ranghild of Rungmook, who won her third CC in 1912. Her dam, Rubina of Rungmook, was the winner of two CCs and was "the first blue bitch to attract attention in this country. Bred from comparatively unknown parents, she created quite a sensation when brought out by Miss Dickinson after winning everything locally at Birmingham. She is a dark-blue with big bone, and has a square deep muzzle, good body, brisket and hindquarters."

One of the first breeders of blues was Mr Milstead and, upon his death, Miss Dickinson bought Prince of Osterstein from his kennel, who unfortunately died young. Rubina had lines back to the brindle and fawn Redgraves, as well as two to the harlequin Ch. Ronald of Redgrave. Rangild "has hardly a white hair, and is very tall, with good legs and feet. She has a long level head, fine skull, a good expression and is an excellent mover."

Harlequins were in a healthy state in the years up to the First World War. Ch. Fortuna of Lockerbie was the winner of eleven CCs and also won in variety competition, including best bitch all breeds at the Kennel Club's own show. She was considered "a beautiful animal at any time when in form, but when seen in the ring in the best condition it is difficult to rate her too highly." It was also said that she could compete with the best that Germany could offer at that time.

The last pre-war Champion, made up in 1917 (for showing did not stop until that year), was Mrs Hornsby's harlequin, Ch. Sandra of Looe. Though Championship dog shows continued through the first three years of the war, strict regulations were introduced so that dogs born from that year until 1919 were ineligible for registration. Ch. Sandra was the winner of seventeen CCs, and was a granddaughter of the influential imported harlequin sire, Greenhill Squire, who was also the sire of Ch. Zenda of Sudbury, the first of Mrs Hatfield's Sudbury Champions, followed by Zarang, Zarina and Zinona.

THE TWENTIES AND THIRTIES
After the First World War, the breeding of Great Danes continued with the customary dedication and enthusiasm, but with a very important extra – money! Two gentlemen, both millionaires, carved their way into the history of the breed – Mr J.V.Rank of the Ouborough Great Danes, and Gordon Stewart of the Send Great Danes. Between 1921 and 1936 these gentlemen imported no less than eighty-six of the finest quality Danes, mainly from Germany.

Most Great Danes in Britain today can be traced back to Ouborough and Send breeding. Between the wars these two great kennels dominated the scene. One of the advantages was W.G.Siggers, kennel manager for the Ouborough kennel. Bill Siggers' natural talent as a stockman, and his supreme skill as a handler ensured continued success for this large kennel. Champions were produced consistently, and approximately thirty Champions carried the Ouborough prefix.

The Send kennel achieved enormous fame not only for quality Danes, but for the sheer size and splendour of the kennel, which was understood to be one of the biggest breeding establishments in the world, housing several hundred Danes at a time. Photographs are still in existence showing armies of smartly clad kennel-staff, and even greater numbers of Danes. Mr Stewart was keen to have his Danes mentally alert as well as physically in the peak of condition, and displays were given showing the obedience and intelligence of the Sends.

As long as there have been, and as long as there continue to be, dog shows, we regularly hear the complaint of 'faces' winning, with the suggestion that the smaller or newer exhibitor cannot get past the established and known kennels and their Danes, never stopping to think that often the 'faces' have the best Danes! Let all those who complained about the strength and successes of kennels like Oldmanor and Moonsfield, and later, Dicarl and Walkmyll, just stop to think how it must have been to compete against Ouborough and Send! But some did, and if their Danes were good enough, they got through, just as they always have and always will. Mrs Hatfield's Sudbury harlequins were joined by the Trayshills of Mrs Lee Booker, and the Rufflyn, Aywell, Arnoldsfield, Canis Major, and Cuckmere kennels were all active and competing against the two giants in the breed.

The year 1930 saw a Champion with a prefix you may find in your Dane's pedigree if you go far enough back – the first Blendon Champion, Bedina. Muriel Osborn was to be a part of the breed for the following fifty years, joined in time by Doris Tittle. The Blendons achieved worldwide fame; the ladies were much loved and eventually began the Midland and West of England Great Dane Club, giving encouragement to so many young Dane enthusiasts – including me! – and first introducing the Dane Rescue scheme, displaying love and concern for the breed.

Prior to the outbreak of the Second World War, the breed was in a healthy state, there were 120 registered breeders of Great Dane, and two more Breed Clubs emerged – the Northern Great Dane Club and the Great Dane Breeders Association. Interest was high, the Great Dane had never been in a stronger and healthier position – and then came the war.

THE WAR YEARS

I learned a great deal from Dibbie Somerfield (daughter of Mrs Booker), owner of the Panfield Boxers, a breed in which I have always been interested. Dibbie would make us both weep with stories of the hardships suffered by Great Danes and their owners during the war years. Imagine trying to find food for a kennel of Great Danes in times of shortage. When breeders have been forced to disband their stock, to have healthy dogs put to sleep, to fail their dogs in some way or another through no fault of their own, even by lack of petrol to get them to a veterinarian for help when needed – after all that heartbreak, how do they begin again when times are better? The 'heart' had gone from many Dane breeders and understandably so. The war had taken its toll.

AFTER THE SECOND WORLD WAR

However, the next generation, with guidance from the few remaining experienced breeders, did begin to return the Great Dane to its former splendour. Mr J.V.Rank had been able to keep a small number of his Ouborough Danes going, Muriel Osborn had kept her strain alive. Mrs Hatfield had lost her son, and due to her own advancing years she gave up her famous Sudbury kennel. Miss M.Lomas took on the harlequin banner with her Wideskies, and John Silver was taken by the same colour and established his Silvernia Danes. Blues and blacks had perhaps suffered the most severe setbacks and they were all but extinct until a young Nellie Ennals breathed new life into them, making Champions in both colours, as well as in fawns – and so Bringtonhill was born.

Gladys Clayton using an Ouborough sire, Rebellion, bred the first bitch to gain her title after the war. This was a lovely fawn, Ch. Bon Adventure Of Barvae. Today's showgoers may not realise that Patricia Clayton who awards CCs regularly in our breed is, in fact,

Gladys Clayton's daughter. Connie Robb of Foxbar was based in Scotland, and she made up Ch. Royalism Of Ouborough. However, the first Great Dane Champion male after the war was Mrs Rowberry's Ch. Juan Of Winome, a prefix that bred on successfully for many years.

The first Great Dane Club Championship Show after the War was in 1946, and the judge was Gordon Stewart. Ch. Juan went Best of Breed and the Bitch CC went to Kitty Guthrie's Moundpine Of Maspound. Mr Rank's Ch. Royalism Of Oughborough became the dominant sire of the time with no fewer than eleven Champion offspring to his credit.

FAMOUS GREAT DANES

Breeders' thoughts turned to the quality stock in other countries, and Mr Rank brought in from Germany a handsome male called Hector Of Ouborough. Mr Rank decided on this fellow's name, as when he arrived, he didn't have one – not a pedigree name anyway, nor any papers. What he did have was obvious good breeding behind him. Starting as an army mascot, he became, when his regiment was disbanded, perhaps the most famous grandsire of all time.

His grandson was Ch. Elch Elder Of Ouborough. With Bill Siggers as handler, this Dane achieved something no other Dane, before or since, has ever achieved. He went Best In Show at Crufts in 1953. Sadly, neither Mr Rank or Mr Stewart were alive to see 'their' breed take the top title of all. However, some Ouboroughs continued for more years, achieving more glory with Bill in the driving seat.

Muriel Osborn had also imported a fawn male. Fingards King Of Kings Of Blendon was brought in from Toronto, Canada, and he became a notable sire. His successes included a grandson, Ch. Bonhomie Of Blendon, who was the only Dane ever to beat the famous Elch in the show ring.

THE FIFTIES AND SIXTIES

The fifties is remembered as the decade in which a Great Dane went Best in Show at Crufts. 1953 was indeed a golden year. Two kennels that went on to be the most influential kennels of the breed, made up their first Champions – Ch. Imogen Of Oldmanor and Ch. Tandye Of Moonsfield. The Oldmanor prefix belonged to the Rev. Gwynn and Olive Davies, although Olive's mother had originated the kennel before the war. Moonsfield belonged to Edna Harrild, and her kennel was was formed in 1940.

Both kennels consistently produced Champions for the next twenty years; both kennels had prepotent stud dogs who were widely used; both kennels bred and sold Champions for others' enjoyment, not only their own; both kennels provided foundation stock for the successful breeders of the coming years; and, without doubt, both kennels are an integral part of the breed's history. A great debt is owed to both these knowledgeable and determined ladies and their backroom boy or kennel-lad husbands!

Olive and Edna were 'the breed' to my generation, although we dare not call them by christian name until permission was given! Olive had the strongest personality – still does! She was a great 'stockman' and managed a kennel of maybe forty Great Danes, all milling around together in a huge yard. She was the pack-leader, she was the boss! Her Danes were

The beautiful Ch. Oldmanor Manthem of Auldmoor, shown here with owner Ann Foxwell and the late L.C.James.

Gerald Foyle.

Endroma French Connection: A representative of the successful Endroma kennel.

Diane Pearce.

Ch. Moonsfield Tellora, owned by the late Mrs Ida Wheeler.   *Ann Cumbers.*

Great! Edna, who sadly died just before her eightieth birthday, was far more laid back, and until you knew her well, she appeared to be an off-hand character. In friendship, however, she was wonderful, and her interest and commitment to true breed type made her irresistible to new breed fanciers. Her Danes were great!

The breed was full of competitive characters and good Great Danes at this time. Joan Kelly – and the beautifully marked Leesthorphill harlequins – is unforgettable with her tweed suits, 'proper' hats, and hand-rolled gold-embossed cigarettes – rolling up at shows in a Mercedes, while her kennelman, Walter, who had been her husband's batman in the war, arrived with a horsebox full of harlequins.

Ch. Walkmyll Montgomery: A fine, upstanding male, bred by Freda Lewis of the Walkmyll kennel – one of the most influential kennels of its era.

The Clausentum kennel was owned by Hilda Lanning and her daughter Jean, who went on to become an authority on the breed, writing books and becoming a world-famous all-round judge. Their first Champion was Ch. Challenger Of Clausentum, made up in 1956. Also in that year Jean Cameron made up Ch. Flambonetta Of Billil, bred by the henna-haired, chain-smoking Lillian Isaacs, who bred such quality, well-balanced Danes – they just could not stand wrong! Jean bred some very good moving Danes; how we all loved Ch. Soraya Of Nightsgift.

Captain and Mrs Hutton were of Merrowlea fame, and fame it was, as their number of Champions was accompanied by a great advertising campaign stressing the great size of these impressive dogs. In 1965 Freda Lewis made up her first Dane, Ch. Walkmyll Moonyean Of Edzell, and Walkmyll Champions came thick and fast over the next couple of decades. Aysdaine, Endroma, Alvenor, Timellie, Kontiki, Impton, Gaymiles, Kilcroney, Beechfields, Gowerfield, Helmlake, and Dicarl are just some of the well-known prefixes that, together with the existing famous names, took the breed onwards.

THE CHANGING SCENE
I suppose it is natural that any breeder remembers their own era with the most affection – and concern. Certainly during the sixties, seventies and eighties, the show rings were full of British-bred, typical, quality Danes, provided by breeders whose admiration of the kennels of the past ensured that consistency of type was maintained.

But the winds of change were also blowing, and a variety of Danes from various Continents were imported into Britain and used extensively at stud, culminating in changes in the basic shape, type and quality of the overall picture of the breed in Britain. The breed became virtually divided into those who maintained loyalty to the Great Dane as we knew it, the 'British' Dane, and those who fell for the allure of the 'import' type. Fresh bloodlines,

Ch. Batworth Bombadier: Cleverly bred by Bob Otoo and Matti Pakerinen to combine bloodlines of British and imported stock.

American import Danelagh's Euros of Walkmyll: One of the first of the extensively used imports. His influence was widely seen.

Ron Lewis.

wisely used, are of benefit to any breed. And so it was in Britain! Imported dogs used indiscriminately, without knowledge of pedigree or ancestry and simply because they are 'new', can cause untold damage to any breed and its future. And so it was in Britain!

INFLUENTIAL IMPORTS

Those of us who spent our formative years in the sixties and seventies had based our kennels on stock from the greats of that time, who were gradually moving aside to make way for the next generation. Carrying us into the seventies, the stud dogs of great note were Ch. Moyalism Of Oldmanor (a son of Oldmanor Tattoo Of Moonsfield), Ch. Telaman of Moonsfield, Ch. Oldmanor Pioneer Of Daneii (a Moyalism son), and Ch. Fergus Of Clausentum.

Fergus was born in 1967, bred by Hilda and Jean Lanning, sired by the imported Clausentum Danelaghs Quillan from Nancy Carol Draper's famous American kennel. Quillan was the result of a half-brother and sister mating to the great American male, Ch. Dinro Taboo. His son was used wisely and well, and he sired Champions not only for the Clausentum kennel but also for Girlie and Tim Harms-Cooke, with Ch. Timellie Caspian and for Karina and Gordon Le Mare with Ch. Simba of Helmlake; his litter sister, Ch. Malindi, and his son, Ch. Walkmyll Kastor of Clausentum, owned by Freda Lewis. Kastor, in turn, sired Ch. Walkmyll Storm, who, as well as having a great show career, sired Champions for Freda Lewis, Elaine and David Parish, and Ann Foxwell (formerly Harris).

Elaine and Ann both began with beautiful Oldmanor Champion bitches, and they

The Batworth kennel produced Champions in three colours. This harlequin bitch is Ch. Batworth Pachino, expertly handled by Matti Pakerinen.

Ch. Dorneywood Orestes: One of the many Champions bred by Elaine and David Parish. Orestes' sister was the much-admired Ch. Dorneywood Opium.

Diane Pearce.

developed their kennels with imported stock to high levels of success. Elaine sensibly helped everyone to follow the Dorneywood Champions with the use of names in alphabetical order. Ch. Infanta followed Ch. Electra, who followed Ch. Damask and others – but you've got the picture! Ann tended to go with 'A' for her name choices, and Champions Achaea and Arianne, along with other Auldmoors enjoyed spectacular show careers.

Freda Lewis brought another dog in from America who was to have a tremendous influence on the breed, Danelaghs Euros of Walkmyll, who sired ten Champions including three in one litter for the Stranahan prefix, owned by John and Thelma Reay.

The other import of the seventies to have far-reaching impact on the breed was Lincoln's Winstead Von Raseac, purchased by Sheila and Brian Edmonds of the Sherain kennel. On Sherain-bred bitches he sired Champions for the Salpetra kennel, owned by Sally and Peter Anders. Joy and Ivan Butcher mated him to their Daneton Princess and bred the top winning Dane, Ch. Daneton Amelia, owned by Mr and Mrs Mike Duckworth. But it is to his first Champion son we should look for continuing influence.

In 1980 Ch. Samani Desert Chief gained his title at a tender age. He was bred by Betty Bacon from a lovely and well-bred Samani bitch, and he quickly found fame as a stud dog as well as in the show ring. Miss A.Hartley and Mrs S.Holmes used him on an Auldmoor bitch, and Ch. Picanbil Pericles became a handsome, much-admired brindle Champion. His sister was Ch. Arianne Of Auldmoor. For Wyn Doyle he sired Ch. Daneways Dolly Clothes

Peg, and in 1986 he sired the first of the Yacanto Champions, Ch. Yacanto Tudor Melody for Dianne and Mike Bousfield. In all, Desert Chief had ten Champion offspring to his credit.

The Helmlake kennel has enjoyed continual winning in that most difficult colour of all, harlequin (as well as victories with fawns and brindles, of course). While Joan Kelly's Leesthorpehill Danes had pleased with general quality, markings and type, Karina Le Mare brought in more size, substance and fresh vigour with the importation of Helmlake Ben El Eick Von Forellen Paradies. The first time I saw this great-boned giant of a dog, he was throwing around a huge tyre in a tennis court which served as his play area. He passed his tremendous strength and substance on to his son, Ch. Helmlake Chico, whose daughter, Ch. Helmlake Fancy Fashion in turn whelped Ch. Helmlake Implicable, sire of Ch. Helmlake Next In Line.

The Impton kennel of Margaret Everton has a success story all its own. Margaret has now retired from breeding and exhibiting, and she has taken her place as an all-rounder judge in a busy schedule that includes the Secretaryship of an All Breeds Championship Show. Not limited by colour preference, Margaret had Champions in fawn, brindle, blue and black – a rare achievement – although range of colour success must be noted in the Endroma and Batworth kennels.

Clever use was made of British lines in Sarzec and Merrowlea, and first-hand knowledge of foreign bloodlines ensured wise importing of Airways and Harmony Hill bred stock. There were spectacular achievements with the brindle male, Ch. Airways Wrangler Of Impton, bred by one of the most respected Dane authorities worldwide, Ulla Magnusson, from Sweden. His use was not restricted to the show ring; he was another import to sire an Auldmoor Champion, as did another Airways import in later years. Wrangler also sired Champions for the Kontiki and Valkyr Danes.

In 1973 the black littermates from Sweden, Ch. Impton Duralex Bernando and Ch. Impton Duralex Burnita were campaigned and taken to great heights, Bernando taking Best in Show at an All Breed Championship Show.

ESTABLISHED BRITISH LINES

In spite of the influx of imported stock, established type held during the seventies into the eighties. Oldmanor and Moonsfield Danes won CCs in the early seventies, and stock bred through those lines took the lion's share well into the eighties.

1970 saw the first Champion bred by Audrey Sheppard, Ch. Gowerfield Candy Caress Of Aysdaine, owned by her friend, Aeron Clement, who later knew the joy of breeding Champions for Audrey with Ch. Gowerfield Galestorm Of Aysdaine, and for Ann Heaton who owned Ch. Gowerfield Gilden. Ann is now Mrs Clive Lunt, and she shared Clive's pleasure in campaigning Ch. Calbren Duck And Dive With Dicarl.

In 1971 Nellie Ennals made up another Champion in the fawn, Telaman-sired male, Ch. Steed Of Bringtonhill. Timellie and Walkmyll (before the addition of imported stock, as well as after) were always amongst the top winners. By the mid-seventies and through the eighties, the Dicarl Dane featured strongly. If a Great Dane was of sufficient merit, it did get to the top, regardless of breeding, ownership or handler. Ch. Laburmax Eurydice, Ch.

Ch. Gowerfield Candy Caress: A bitch of great type and quality. Bred by Audrey Sheppard and owned by Aeron Clement.

Audrey Sheppard with her daughter Alaine and Four Aysdaine Great Danes. Showgoers of the sixties remember Alaine as a toddler reared with Danes. Now she shares in running this much-respected kennel.

Ch. Gowerfield Galestorm of Aysdaine: A dog that was greatly admired for his correct conformation and breed type. Sire of Ch. Dicarl The Heavyweight, his place in history is assured.

Diane Pearce.

Wykendrift Marcellus, Ch. Brutondane Delblonde, Ch. Faircrest Easter Wish, Ch. Tarus Major Concession, Ch. Vernlam Maxie Of Delwin, Ch. Millpark Kreme Kracker, Ch. Ashville Harvey and Ch. Falconburg Arcas are all examples of novices in the breed reaching the heights without the benefit of being a known 'face' or having a famous kennel name – providing, of course, the owner has the time and resources necessary; for showing dogs is a time-consuming and costly hobby.

THE SHOW SYSTEM
The strength of a kennel lies not only in its ability to breed and make up Champions for itself, but to produce dogs of merit consistently and to be prepared and happy to see others win with them. A book of this kind can only scratch the surface, and only those with that magic title of Champion seem to be of importance. An average entry of Great Danes at a Club or Championship Show is between 150 to 250 Danes, and only two of those can win a CC.

The kennels deserving the most respect are those whose breeding features throughout the classes, and that is dependent upon number of resident inmates, numbers of litters bred, and the good fortune to sell puppies to people who wish to show, thereby keeping that particular kennel name to the fore. In Great Britain the competition is always strong, as a nucleus of the best Danes at any time will be at any show. There is no 'easy' way for a Dane to win

Ch. Dicarl The Beguiling: A bitch of quality and breed type.

Ch. Dicarl Who's Free: One on a long line of Dicarl Champions.

CCs; a dog will always have to beat other top winners; even at the far-flung shows, such as Scotland and Paignton, some top Danes will be there keeping CCs elusive – and worth all the more for being so.

It takes great perseverance to make a Champion. Some breeders never or rarely achieve the accolade. That does not mean they have not bred good, sound typical stock over the years. There have been Danes always 'in the Cards', placed above most of the top-winning Danes on occasions and yet never capturing a CC. Others can win first placings on certain days and take the CC, where at the majority of shows they go cardless.

About thirty years ago, Gwen Herbert and I both bought £100 worth of Premium Bonds. Every three months when the numbers were drawn, Gwennie won something! Perhaps only £25 or £50 – but something! Thirty years on, I still haven't ever won anything on those Premium Bonds! But how unlucky Gwennie was not to make Algywnne Mountain Echo a Champion, and how lucky I was with the winning of the Dicarls. The element of luck is always involved!

NEW ENTHUSIASTS OF THE SEVENTIES
The seventies were good years for new enthusiasts to the breed. They included: Sylvia and Geoff Burton of Devarro, Jean and Jack Taylor of Enydelet, Tony and Helen Pearce of Anset, Frances and Jack Krall of Jafrak, and many others who gave their time and enthusiasm for the future of the breed.

Sylvia and Geoff Burton bred three commanding, impressive brindle males including Ch. Devarro Direct Descendant, who was used extensively at stud. Jean and Jack Taylor seem to have the happy knack of making up the Danes they choose to campaign – from the first, Ch. Enydelet Pandora Beauty in 1978 and her daughter, Ch. Enydelet The Madam in 1980, to the latest Champion, who took Best of Breed at Crufts in 1992, Ch. Foxwood Forte Du Enydelet, bred by Norma and Wayne Rylance.

Anset and Jafrak produced Champions, and typical Great Danes of quality and substance were bred by the newer and smaller kennels of Jalus, Eastlight, Spearmount, Janriche, and many others. The Heavyweight and The Weightlifter were the dogs most finding favour at stud by those who wished to keep to type as established by the Oldmanor and Moonsfield Great Danes.

THE END OF THE EIGHTIES
By the end of the eighties the Great Dane scene in Great Britain had changed to an alarming degree. The flood of imports, the lack of strong line-bred kennels, the divergence of opinion among breeders and judges as to what actually makes a Dane Great, resulted in show ring classes that could be seen as 'Any Variety Great Dane'. Although all were bred and registered as Great Danes, and were, of course, appreciated by certain sections of the fancy, it was sometimes difficult to believe that these large dogs of assorted shapes and sizes were actually all the same breed!

The 'old-fashioned type' had been a term used as a compliment for Great Danes possessing the conformation and appearance of recognisable qualities developed over the years, but it now became a dismissive insult used by those of the 'new' wave who required a different and 'modern' look to their Danes and pedigrees containing foreign bloodlines in abundance.

Clausentum Danelaghs Quillan had been used sensibly by the Lannings. He was mated to a bitch of their breeding, and the son, Ch. Fergus Of Clausentum, was used on British-bred bitches and the offspring mated back into British-bred lines, thereby maintaining type but bringing in fresh vigour and accompanying virtues. Members of the new wave, with less grasp of the basics of good breeding, had used any new dog or bitch on arrival in this country and taken the next generation, not back into a line, but on to yet another outcross Dane imported from probably an entirely different Continent.

The kennels housing the dominant line-bred stud dogs, such as Oldmanor, Moonsfield and Dicarl had retired, and the breed was wide open for the next generation to have their way. Experienced guidance was lacking, or certainly not sought by the newer breeders and judges, and the result was the wide diversity of type and shape we saw in the show rings by the end of the eighties. This was truly the end of a great era in the history of the Great Dane in Great Britain.

ON TO THE NINETIES

Enthusiasm for the breed remains high, and numerically the strength holds. Whatever the appearance of the Great Dane, good temperament remains constant. Great bone and substance are still achieved and the heads of Danes in the nineties are, overall, impressive.

Some famous kennels of the past keep the involvement. Jean Cameron of the wonderful Nightgifts was joined by Julie and Tony Schanning-Ling; Rae and Peter Russell continue to breed the Endromas; Gwen and Alan Herbert together with their son, Les, still exhibit typical Great Danes, as do Audrey Sheppard and her daughter, Alaine, as well as several of

Ch. Yacanto This Is Sunny: A daughter of Top Gun, with a notable show career. She is pictured winning the Working Group at Midland Counties Championship Show under Andrew Thompson, with breed judge Miki Ramsey and Ann Foxwell presenting the trophy.

Russell Fine Art.

Ch. Endroma Leopold: A blue male of good breed type   Carol Ann Johnson.

Ch. Yacanto Cuddley Duddley At Abacus winning a Reserve Group placing at the Manchester Championship show from judge, Jack Bispham. Bred by Diane and Michael Bousfield, owned by Mrs C. Coombes.

Ch. Batworth Obsession At Marridane: An outstanding harlequin bitch.   *Diane Pearce.*

Ann Foxwell continues her winning ways, ably assisted by her son, Jeff Horswell, who often handles this youngster, Auldmoors American Honey.   *Diane Pearce.*

the breeders already mentioned. They include Freda Lewis and Karina Le Mare – and Betty Bacon is still winning with her Samani Danes. Rosalie and Elwyn Cobley have bred Champions in fawn and black with the Eleeta prefix. The Auldmoors, Gemfloras, and Batworths continue to breed.

The Yacanto kennel has proved its strength in a succession of Champions and has closely aligned the Garsak kennel of Gary Hooker and John Lockey. These kennels have mastered the art of presentation and reaped the rewards. Jennie Roberts and her Arondyke Danes, and Sue Yule Pollock with Bencleves still regularly exhibit. The newer kennels of Nigel Marriner and Elaine Harrison support the harlequin with the Marridane prefix, and Champions include the Top Dane of 1991, Ch. Batworth Obsession For Marridane, bred by Bob Otto and Matti Pakerinen. It would, of course, be impossible to mention all the Great

Epitomising the nineties: Gary Hooker and Ch. Garsak Sir Galahad – a top handler and a top Dane. This kennel has enjoyed phenomenal success.

Michael Trafford.

Ch. Devarro Fine And Brandy: A representative of the Devarro Great Danes.

Diane Pearce.

Danes and their owners and breeders who deserve a mention in any attempted history of the breed. Space does not permit, and memory does not always function, but tribute should be paid, dedication recognised, and commitment appreciated.

While my opinion of the majority of the show Great Danes of the nineties in Britain may not be terribly high in regard to type and quality, I am well aware of the love and care that goes into them and can wholeheartedly congratulate today's owners on the condition of the show dogs. Would that there was a closer relationship between the breeders, as only by talking together and comparing opinions can the devotees learn from and teach each other.

There are now nine Great Dane Breed Clubs in Britain, all of value, yet sometimes serving to divide the Dane world. The objective of every club and every breeder should be the same: the breed and its welfare. There can be no doubt about the continuing popularity of the Great Dane in Britain, and those of us with an interest in the breed can only hope that, if and when another breed book is written in ten, twenty or thirty years' time, there will be a chapter included on the astounding improvements in the breed during the nineties and into the 21st Century!

Chapter Nine

THE GREAT DANE IN NORTH AMERICA

Inevitably, a country admired for its size and splendour, would take to its heart a breed possessing similar attributes. The Great Danes of America have been appreciated, and, in fact, been the envy of breed fanciers throughout the world. American professionalism and publicity 'know-how' have ensured the visibility of the American Dane to the rest of the world. The many excellent books on the breed, the breathtaking glossy magazines, and the well travelled American Dane breeders have provided constant photographic evidence of the breed's excellence on that great continent.

Brilliant handlers and superb photographers have enhanced the noble breed, and, perhaps, have shamed and intimidated those from other countries, where 'happy snaps' are more the norm! A snapshot taken in a small garden with the Brownie 127 can hardly compare with those colourful, flower-decked show-winning photographs at which the Americans excel. So, of course, we all drool over the American Great Danes. They are splendid – and there are so many! It is such a vast continent, and in a typical month *The American Kennel Gazette* recently listed 241 litters registered, for a total of 846 individual Great Dane puppies.

Any successful and level-headed American Great Dane breeder will confirm that there are wonderful Great Danes in the USA – and there are those that are not so wonderful. There is but one breed Standard, but individual breeders' interpretations' of that Standard has produced a wide variance of type across the country. Similar remarks can apply to any country, but, of course, not on such a grand scale. However, there can be no doubt of the dedicatied commitment and the financial commitment, of the American Great Dane breeder over the last one hundred years or so.

EARLY HISTORY

In 1889 the Great Dane Club of America was formed. Previously Danes had been exhibited as Boarhounds under the Ulm Dog heading, and even in Siberian Bloodhound classes! The American Kennel Club had no doubts about the breed's true name, and the first Great Dane Champion listed in their records was a brindle bitch, Juno, owned by the Osceola kennel of Wisconsin. This bitch was bred in Germany in 1885 by Count Hilliger of Berlin. The Osceola kennel had the distinction of also owning the second Champion in the breed. This was Don Caesar, a fawn male born in Prussia in 1886, bred by Otto Friedrich. At the Westminster Kennel Club Show of 1887 Don Caesar took Best of Breed.

However, it was not until 1889 that the AKC accepted and formulated the first American Standard for the breed. It is estimated that at this time, and during the next twenty years or so, the breed was under the firm control of some twenty to twenty-five breeders across the country, breeders who had the financial resources to maintain kennels 100-200 strong and were prepared to invest heavily in the importation of top-quality animals, mainly from German kennels.

Up to 1900, fourteen Champions were recorded, mainly brindles, with one fawn and two harlequins. The next ten years saw forty-four Danes gaining their titles, with the brindle coloration finding favour, although the two listed as 'blue brindle' and 'white slate' cause concern. It may be charitable to suggest that breeders in those days were more concerned about conformation and breed type than colour!

These early breeders, whose aims for the breed were so high, with scant regard for their pockets, continued with the advancement of the Great Dane in America. In 1908 The Great Dane Club of America staged a show at which ninety-nine Danes paraded for the perusal of a top German judge and breeder, Herr Fritz Kirschbaum. The breed was well established and gaining in popularity. From 1920 to 1935, 163 Great Danes gained the title of Champion, and of those, seventy-eight were imports.

The great and famous names of kennels and Danes of those years are part of breed history and record, and modern breeders still acknowledge the debt owed to those committed breeders. Some of the Danes of those times are legendary, and they are still talked of today with reverence by famous judges. Those who saw the great Ch. Etfa von de Saalburg have her high on their list of best dogs ever – any breed! Her photograph confirms this. She was magnificent, beautifully constructed with quality and substance, as were so many of that era. The Brae Tarn kennel of R.P. Stevens of Connecticut had so many great imports and so many excellent homebred Danes – what a lasting tribute that a kennel discontinued in 1941 is remembered with awe some fifty years later!

THE GREAT BREEDERS

It would take an American specialist to give suitable accolade to the dogs and breeders of those times. From a distance my view was limited, but those I particularly admired were: Ch. Senta, Gregory Of Kent, Ch. Honey Hollow Stormi Rudio, Ch. Big Kim Of Bella Dane, Ch. Lane Turn Burgundy, Ch. Its Mellow Of Marydane, Ch. Dion Of Kent, Ch. Tallbrooks Bit O'Honey, and Hora Doggensport (I was sure I could have bred Champions from her!).

Danes from Dane Eden, Lane Turn, Dinros, Meistersingers, and Honey Hollow all impressed – great Danes, great breeders, great handlers, all caught the imagination of my generation of British Great Dane breeders. Naturally, Britain had its own stars and personalities. Bill Siggers was kennel manager and handler for the great Ouborough kennel. He handled Ch. Elch Elder of Ouborough to Best In Show at Crufts, and he went on to become a much-loved and highly respected all-rounder judge. Bill's personality and character made him a legend – to many he was Mr Great Dane. Across the Atlantic, America had Lina Basquette! Lina epitomized, to the rest of the world, the glamour and

Ch. Brier Rika Injun Spirit Chany: The top Great Dane bitch of 1992.

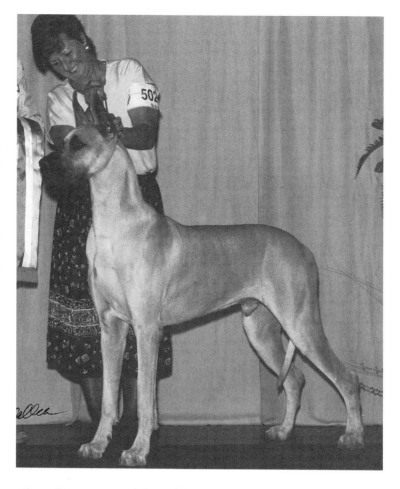

BIS BISS Am. Can. Int. Ch. Amelor's Fly So Free: A son of the legendary BIS BISS Ch. Von Shrado's I'm A Knockout (bred by Art Melio out of Amelor's Encore), owned by Lisa Deroulet and Mark Vanalsyne, handled by Louise Vanalsyne. In 1992 he graded No.4 in the Great Dane Group Systems.

excitement of the American Great Dane scene. A beautiful and vivacious young actress, she became a top breeder and handler, possessing the style and ring presence we sought to achieve in our Great Danes. A magical lady who is still turning heads and looking gorgeous in maturity. Age and experience bring things into proportion, but it does not lessen factual achievements or diminish interest in those great Danes of the past.

PRESENT-DAY KENNELS

American kennels of today that earn respect by their consistent breeding of quality Great Danes include: Honey Lane, Dagon, Rojon, Von Raseac, Dinro-Sounda, Riverwood, Ranch, Lincoln, Longo, Shadam, Von Shrado, Sandale, Don-Lu, Warwick, Sheenwater, and many, many more.

THE SHOW SCENE

Up to the sixties Great Danes in America were shown pretty much in their own area, rarely attending a show more than 400-500 miles away. There was very little breeding between the

Ch. Patchwork's Ashley Wilkes: BOB at the GDCA National Specialty in 1990. He is handled by the well-known Dick Schaefer, who clearly forms a special relationship with his charges.

Missy Yuhl.

East Coast, Mid-West and West Coast. With the advent of large jet planes, which were able to accommodate Dane-size crates, with frequent flights to every medium and large city, all this changed. Currently, some Great Dane Champions, in the quest for that Top Dog title, are shown somewhere in the country every weekend of the year.

Of great importance to breeding plans is the fact that distance is not now a hindrance to breeding to a desired stud dog. The days of the large breeding kennel have long gone, as they have in all countries. There are lines that consistently produce Champions, but few have facilities for great numbers of dogs – few have more than a dozen Danes in kennels of the nineties.

Most exhibitors have, perhaps, from two to four Danes who live in their homes. The station-wagons that Dane owners have driven for many years to carry their dogs to shows have been replaced by many breeders and owners with large motorhomes, averaging 36ft. in length. The dogs and owners can rest in air-conditioned or, as the case may be, in warm comfort, between the breed and Group judging at local Shows. For the weekend circuits, far from home, they provide a luxury hotel room for the Danes and their families.

The beautiful Ch. Dagon's Truly Fair.

THE GREAT DANE CLUB OF AMERICA

The GDCA was founded in 1889 and is still going strong more than a century later, but it has moved with the times. For many years the club held their annual Futurity and Specialty in conjunction with the Westchester KC on the East Coast of America, making a long and arduous trip for those exhibitors from the Mid-West and West Coast. In recent years, the GDCA Futurity and National Specialty has been held in a different area of the country each year – obviously a thoughtful and popular change. Winning Best of Breed at the National is every owner's dream. As of 1992, the Top Twenty Competition has been presented by the GDCA. The club does not restrict activities to the beauty show ring – Obedience, agility and flyball events are also part of the curriculum, proving, as we devotees know well, Great Danes are not just pretty faces! The club produces Year Books at very reasonable prices, and is to be commended for a publication they urge breeders and clubs to have freely available, entitled *Before You Choose A Great Dane.*

In a country the size of America, there are, of course, many regional Breed Clubs and details of clubs can be obtained from the AKC or be found listed in the breed's own glossy magazine, *The Great Dane Reporter.*

TOP GREAT DANES

Those of us who choose to show our Danes are, by definition, competitive. This holds from the first outing with a new puppy, where we hope for the pup's participation and enjoyment, envious looks from the opposition, and approval from the judge of the day, to the satisfying day when our pride and joy gains the title of Champion. Is that the time an exhibitor rests on his laurels? Not a bit of it – and certainly not in America.

I have chosen just one American Great Dane to illustrate what can be achieved – this is 'Brother', the Top Great Dane of 1991. This Dane was bred and owned by Carol Ann McKenna and Robert and T.E.Layne. He was sired by Ch. Beaucedane's Gent Jr v Mt Dania out of Ch. Dinro Desiree McKenna, and handled by E.Lyon. Brother became Am. Puerto Rican, South American Champion of the Americas, Multiple BISS Champion Dinro McKenna's Against All Odds.

He won 310 Best of Breeds, 286 Group Placements, 23 Independent Specialty wins, Two-Time Top Producer, Westminster Kennel Club Breed Winner, Multiple International Champion, Top 20 Contender for three consecutive years, No.1 in 1991 – and as if that is not enough, he became Companion and Visitation Dog.

The competitive spirit urges us on. It is never enough to own one of the best Great Danes. We strive to achieve the best of the best. The very best feel the need to compete against each other – and what wonderful viewing that makes for the spectators!

THE TOP TWENTY COMPETITION

In 1987, Dr Louis Bond and Robert Layne, the holders of the Dinro kennel name following the sad death of Rose Roberts, inaugurated a Top Twenty Competition. Accurate statistics are compiled for a calendar year on each Great Dane and the number of Danes they have defeated by winning Best of Breed. The Top Twenty Great Danes on this list are invited to compete in a format judged by three judges from the following categories:

Ch. Ba-Ke-Vo's Independent Lady: Winner Top Twenty 1988. Bred and owned by Barbara, Ken and Dee Vos.

1. A breeder judge with at least ten years experience as a breeder, who has bred at least ten Champions of record as published in the *American Kennel Gazette*.
2. A multi-breed AKC-approved judge, qualified to judge Great Danes and at least ten other breeds in any Group.
3. A professional handler, meeting the requirements for membership in the Professional Handlers Association, and with at least ten years experience.

The Danes have to be individually evaluated by each judge, and the winner is determined by computer analysis of each judge's scoring. A win at this event is, of course, something to

Am. Puerto Rican, S. Am. Champion of the Americas, multiple BISS Ch. Dinro McKenna's Against All Odds, known as 'Brother'.

be very proud of. To be a spectator at this event is extremely educational, giving everyone a chance to view the Best of the Best, the cream of the crop, and promoting discussion and exchange of opinions.

In 1987 the winner was a most beautiful fawn bitch, Ch. Dagon's Truly Fair, bred by Barbara A.Vos and owned by Barbara, Dee and Ken Vos. In 1988, another glorious fawn lady, Ch. Ba-Ke-Vo's Independent Lady took honours. This bitch was also bred by Barbara A.Vos and owned by Barbara, Dee and Ken Vos. In 1989, a handsome fawn male, Ch. Sheenwater Gamble On Me, bred and owned by Sally Chandler and Chris O'Connell, won the title. He was, in fact, the Top Great Dane and Top Working Dog in 1987 and has sired

This elegant, stylish brindle is Ch. Alano's Anastasia Of Maitau, who took BOB at the GDCA National Specialty in 1991.

O. Tiademan.

Champions into double figures. In 1990 it was the turn of quality fawn girl, Ch. Rojon's Rumour Has It, bred by Faye and Ringhand Krueger and Ray Cataldi Jr., Blair and Judy Bath and Catherine Most. Rumour had a wonderful show career and was also the No.1 Great Dane in 1989.

A VERY SPECIAL GREAT DANE

There is one very special Great Dane who has been featuring in this prestigious competition since its beginnings – Ch. Von Shrado's I'm A Knockout. This very special fawn boy was whelped on September 7th 1986, and he finished his Championship at ten months. He was Best in Futurity, GDCA at twelve months of age. As already mentioned, he has featured in the Top Twenty rankings for the past six years. In 1990 he was No.1 Dane and No.1 Sire; he repeated those placings in 1992. To date he has sired twenty-six Champions, two Best in Show winners and a Top Twenty Winner.

Known by his pet name 'Fridge', this Dane has won 10 BIS, 22 Specialty BIS, and 404 Best of Breeds, which is an all-time record. Fridge has taken 58 Group firsts, 67 Group seconds, 55 Group thirds, 41 Group fourths – a total of 221 Group placements. He was exhibited at Westminster on one occasion and he took Best of Breed. The judge was Lina Basquette.

What a dog! Let me quote from Sandra and James Hann Jr: "Fridge has been a dream come true for us as breeder, owner, handlers." Of course – but the dream has been the result of hard work and planning. Fridge's dam, and her sire and dam are Von Shrado breeding. The Von Shrado kennel has produced Champions for other people and given them their chance at 'a dream come true'. We can only imagine the amount of work, effort and love that have gone into keeping this male Great Dane in show condition for a six-year period.

OWNER/HANDLERS

Many excellent professional handlers have great success with Danes, but there are also owner/handlers who are well capable of doing the job themselves. Don and Mary Lou Carmody are owner/handlers with a tremendous record. They have had no less that four Best In Show Great Danes: BIS Ch. Mountdania's Ashley, BIS Ch. Don-Lu's Preferred Risk, BIS Ch. Don-Lu's Maggie Davis and BIS Ch. Don-Lu's Just In Time.

Littermates Ch. Kai Dane's Win Ticket (Tina), pictured top, and Ch. Winfall's Bet Twice V. Warwick (David): Both winners of All-breed BIS awards, which is a remarkable feat. Tina was the top Working Dog in Hawaii, 1990. She is owned by Sue Cates and Anne Tooney. David is a great show dog with a most impressive list of wins and is now proving his worth as a sire.

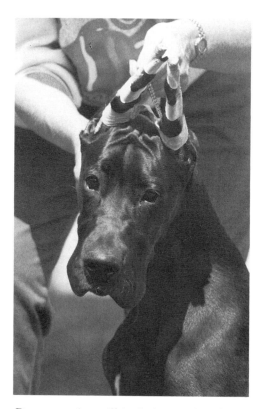

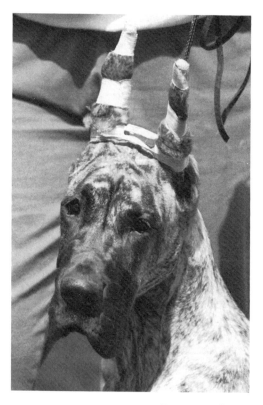

Dane puppies still in their crop bandages.

Lenny Ludham.

Don and Mary Lou have owner/handled twenty-two Champions. Don has said he learned to handle by watching other people and other breeds. He says it's fun, he likes the competition. Don obviously has a natural talent for handling; what is equally obvious, he has worked at it. Success, I have found, is usually deserved.

HISTORY IN THE MAKING

The American Great Danes of today provide strong competition for each other. Those that make the top are ensuring themselves a place in the history of the breed. These are the Great Danes that will be talked of with reverence in years to come. Perhaps none more than Ch. Von Shrado's I'm A Knockout, who is currently still top-winning Dane in breed competition, and also the top-producing sire. Ch. Steigerhill Trail Blazer and Ch. Winfalls Bet Twice of Warwick occupy second and third places in show ring points. Ch. Brier Rika Injun Spirit Chaney is the top-winning bitch, with Ch. Longos Sweetalk of Micheldane and Ch. Gemstones Kaitlyn La-Di-Da following.

The top stud dogs, understandably, bear kennel names that have already carved their way in the breed's history, and following Ch. Von Shrado's I'm A Knockout in the top-producing sire stakes are: Ch. Sandales What A Guy, Ch. Danesfield's Where Eagles Fly,

BIS Ch. Don-Lu's Maggie Davis, bred by Lowell and Arlene Davis. Owner/handled by Don and Mary Lou Carmony.

BIS Mountdania's Ashley, bred by Anna Mary Kauffman and owner/handled by Don and Mary Lou Carmony. Ashley was No.1 Great Dane in 1979 and is also the sire of thirty-six Champions, including Maggie Davis.

BIS Ch. Don-Lu's Just In Time: No.1 Great Dane in 1986. She had a fantastic show career including four All Breed BIS – and she retired at two and a half years old!   *Booth.*

Ch. Sheenwater Gamble On Me, Ch. Von Shrado's I'm A Macho Man, Ch. Dagons In A Flash, Ch. Fireside Agitates Kimdane, Ch. Paquestone's Mistydane Quasar, Ch. Aquino's Rocky of Millcreek, Ch. Brier-Chaney's Judge 'N Jury, Ch. Calico Rock's Frazier Belmont, Ch. Dundane Whistle's At Sharcon, Ch. Longo's Primo D'Aquino, Ch. Orleans Marquis, Ch. Von Graff Dirty Hari of Lost Creek, and Ch. Von Raseacs French Dandy. All Great Danes to be proud of!

THE AMERICAN ATTITUDE

It appears to me that the American Great Dane breeder, owner and exhibitor spares no expense or effort in pursuit of their hobby/lifestyle – call it what you will. Exhibiting a Great Dane is considered a serious business and it is treated accordingly. This does not mean that the sport is not enjoyed – but it is highly competitive. Breeders are fully aware of the need

BIS Ch. Don-Lu's Preferred Risk. This handsome male is a son of Just In Time. He is the winner of three All Breed BIS, and the sire of Champions.

for competent, and more than that, stylish handling. Any Dane is enhanced by clever handling. If the breeder or owner feels they lack a little flair with their Dane on the lead, then they are prepared to pay for the best handler they can find. The enjoyment then comes from seeing their beloved Dane presented to best advantage – and being able to sit back and appreciate the virtues of their stock.

Kennel advertisements are also of a very high standard. They are clearly-worded, entertaining and eye-catching, and always using beautiful photographs – this is something the British could learn a lot from. There is also a more gentle and endearing side to the Dane fanciers' attitude. This is particularly illustrated in the 'In Memory' pages of any American Dane publication. When celebrating the glory of a past Dane or Dane person, there is a real sense of compassion and depth of feeling, which is wholly admirable.

There is also a strong sense of responsibility to the breed, which is notable in publications from the individual breed clubs. For example, *Daneline*, produced by the Great Dane Club of New England is "Dedicated to the Betterment of the Breed." Health and rearing problems are given extensive coverage, all with the aim of encouraging better ownership of this noble breed. It appears to me that a Great Dane puppy with the good fortune to be born in the USA will be presented and promoted to the very best advantage.

THE AMERICAN ADVANTAGE

Let us not beat about the bush – cropped ears! Great Danes look stunning with cropped ears! Erect ears make ordinary heads look good and good heads look even better. In countries where cropping is unacceptable, so knowledge of the procedure is limited, breeders tend to shudder at the very thought of having their pup's ears mutilated, although most are prepared to admit it does look pretty fetching once completed.

Those who do not approve of cropped ears may use the argument that a Great Dane looks kinder and softer with natural ears; there can be a 'fierce' look with the cropped ears. I cannot subscribe to that view. Erect ears make a Dane look more alert and intelligent; the gentle, enquiring, quizzical look comes from the eyes. Erect ears somehow make a Dane look cleaner, the head shape more visible, they accentuate the parallel planes and quality of skull, they enhance a crested neck, they somehow give a Dane more reach and elegance – even nobility.

But they still have to use them properly. Let me quote top American Dane breeder and judge, Jackie White: "When judging, one must choose from what is entered that day – the animal that is best moving, sound of structure, muscle tone and temperament, and with the most breed type. In the USA, with cropped ears on the breed, it is a definite asset to have an animal with an out-going, happy personality, who shows himself off with ears erect." Thank you Jackie, that just about sums it up!

CANADA

There always have been, and always will be, dedicated supporters of Great Danes in Canada. The great size of the country makes competition and comparison extremely difficult. There are five main Great Danes clubs, each serving their own enormous area. The Association of Great Dane fanciers is run from South-Western Ontario. The Great Dane Club of Canada has Ruth Dalton as its secretary, and she resides in the charmingly named Red Deer. Due to its Eastern Ontario location, The Great Dane Club of Quebec is also known as the Club Grand Danois du Quebec. The Midwest Great Dane Club covers Manitoba and Saskatchewan, and the lower mainland is served by the Western Great Dane Club of British Columbia.

The Canadian Great Dane exhibitors do not necessarily have easy path to victory in their show rings as many American Danes cross the border to compete against the local competition. Many splendid Danes carry the dual American and Canadian Championship title with pride. Canada has not been slow to import stock from other countries, not only from the USA – Germany and the UK have also provided bloodlines that have been widely and well used.

INFLUENTIAL BREEDERS

It is appropriate that we look firstly at the Cairndania kennel, owned by Betty Hyslop, as this prefix acquired world fame for Great Danes and Cairn Terriers. Mrs Hyslop's first Champion was in the 1930s, and this was the beautiful Ch. Pax von Birkenhof, a daughter of the famed Etfa vd Saalburg. The brindle Pax also became an American Champion, as, like some of today's exhibitors, Betty Hyslop also faced the competition in the American show rings. Many famous Champions followed, including Am. Can. Ch. Qualga von Lohedie, Am. Can. Ch. Max. of Cairndania, Ch. Senta Hexengold – a quality fawn bitch imported from Germany, where she had been the German Sieger for 1936 – and Can. Am. Ch. Aslan von Lomeland, another Best in Show winner.

While Betty Hyslop was admirably taking care of the brindle and fawn colours, the blues had a champion in the Runmok kennel. This kennel dedicated itself to the cause of the blue Great Dane. It is interesting to note that the blue, black and harlequin colours have been prized by so many Canadian fanciers. In fact, the top-winning Dane of all time in Canada was the handsome, beautifully-marked, quality dog, Am. Can. Ch. Queststar Valdez Of Sheboane, a Best in Show and Best in Specialty Show winner, owner-handled by Bonnie and Gayle Klompstra of Ontario. The Kompstras are successful and dedicated harlequin enthusiasts, and they bred the sire of Valdez, Can. Am. Ch. Sherboane's Johnnie B Goode, who was the first Canadian-bred harlequin Dane in twenty-five years to complete the American Championship.

Valdez, himself, became a most distinguished sire, with ten American Champion offspring to his credit. Owning such good stock, it would have been understandable had the Klompstras decided to rest on their laurels. Not a bit of it! Bonnie travelled to see the Great Danes in Europe, and as a result, Barbel von Harlekin joined the Sherboane kennel. Deserved success continues for the Sherboane Great Danes, and the current star is the beautiful and cleverly-named Can. Ch. Diana-n-Links Dancin In The Dark, again owner-handled by Gayle, and bred by Diana Spring and Guy Link.

TOP DOG, ALL BREEDS

A special mention must be given to Am. Can. Ch. Davos Baroness Zareba. Harmony Hill sired, this elegant brindle bitch, bred by Drs Andy and Sheila Fletch, who won Top Dog, All Breeds in Canada in 1972. The Drs Fletch also bred threat Best in Show inning Ch. Davos Deacon CD TT, who was Top Dane of his year, owned by the Hannadale kennel of Bill and Aila Treloar. Deacon also proved his worth as a sire of Champions, and has the distinction of being the first Great Dane in Canada to be successfully temperament-tested by the American Temperament Test Society. This is most commendable, as breeders must never forget how important temperament is to any breed, and most especially, perhaps, to our gentle giants.

PERSONAL CHOICE

Those of us with a love for this breed spend many hours poring over photographs of Great Danes in different parts of the world. We all know the camera can lie – but how can we resist choosing photochromic favourites? An author can sometimes be allowed a personal view, and the dog that fills my eye is the fawn male, BIS BISS Can. Ch. Boss's First Son Joshua CD TT. According to the photographs I have seen, he has good construction, with a crested neck flowing into a firm, true topline, and well-angulated hindquarters. He pleases me!

He has also found favour in many actual 'hands-on' situations, and one of my favourite photographs shows him Best in Specialty at the Great Dane Club of Canada Show. I see that several of his puppies carry the Lambs Creek prefix, including Can. Ch. Lambs Creek Thorncrest Chimo, a youngster of obvious quality and breed type.

CANADIAN KENNELS
It would be impossible to mention all those who work and strive to breed Great Danes of consistently good breed type. It would be a difficult task for any country, and many good kennels who, perhaps, do not indulge in widespread advertising campaigns may have slipped my attention.

The kennels of Paquestone and Daynakin have asserted a good influence on many of the Danes shown in Canada, and Ch. Paquestone's Mistydane Quasar has certainly made his mark as a stud dog. The Strider kennel and stock of Glen and Kelly Tait has come to my attention, possibly because I have noticed Can. Ch. Boss's First Son Joshua CD TT featuring in their pedigrees. Many Canadian Champions carry the name of Striders in both brindle and fawn colours. Also in these colours, the Whisper Hill kennel, owned by Betty Conod, has a record to be proud of, and I see that her handsome fawn male, Ch. Whisper Hill Tristan took Best in Specialty at the Association of Great Dane Fanciers Show under Bob Heal, who is a regular and welcome visitor to the UK.

It would be wonderful if we could just 'shrink the world' for short periods of time, just long enough so we could see each other's Great Danes. I am sure Canada would provide Many Danes for us to admire.

Chapter Ten

GREAT DANES WORLDWIDE

It would seem that ownership of a Great Dane, even just one family pet, ensures a place in a huge family, a club if you like, of people who share a love and an interest in this breed. Membership extends worldwide – people we may never actually meet and Danes we may see only in photographs become part of conversations creating a common bond between all Dane owners.

Judging dogs has taken me to most parts of the world, and even when the judging assignment is for other breeds, those with an interest in the Great Dane will find a way to talk to me about Danes, discussing how the Danes in their country compare with those in other countries. I am always amazed by the amount of knowledge of happenings in the breed worldwide shown by those in even the most far-flung and unlikely corners of the world.

My generation were most fortunate that Margaret Everton of the Imptons had connections with a coach travel business, and she kindly organised the most wonderful excursions to see the Danes in other countries. Highlights of the seventies were Margaret's 'trips'! Priced well within the pockets of the British Dane fanciers, these luxury coaches took us to all parts of the Continent to see the Dane. Thirty or forty of us, breeders and pet owners, spent long weekends immersed in the breed: during the journeys, the discussions and arguments; during the shows, the exclamations at some of the impressive, often cropped Danes, and the bonus of sometimes visiting kennels and breeders of that country – all part of the learning process that we in the seventies were fortunate enough to be part of.

IN EUROPE

Whatever European country we visited, we were always impressed by the heads on the Danes, enhanced more often than not by cropped ears. Huge shows were staged in Holland, Switzerland, Belgium and Germany, with Danes travelling long distances from adjoining countries to provide spectacles of shows 300, 400, 600 Danes strong, with judging taking place in four or five rings, colours separated, with avid, and noisy, ringsides!

Handling styles were very different to those seen in Britain – single Danes often with as many as three or four handlers and attracters, and sometimes even cats or rabbits displayed ringside in the quest for alertness, dash and daring, so prized in Europe. These Danes may

A beautiful Airways bitch of excellent type. Note her firm topline, good coupling and correct hind angulation.
David Dalton

have 'knocked our eyes out' when standing, with all their strength and majesty, but they often disappointed on the move.

But we were there to learn and enjoy – and how we did! – scouring the trade stands and city shops for Dane models and memorabilia, and returning home with photographs and souvenirs or anything 'Great Dane'.

On one visit to Switzerland I spotted a brindle bitch we liked very much. She was very young, beautifully marked and absolutely teeming with quality. All Dane owners, whatever their nationality, like to have their Danes admired, so after the Class had finished, I went to compliment the young brindle. Imagine my pleasure when the owner suggested I should have my photograph taken with her, as, after all, I had bred her mother! She was the daughter of a fawn bitch I had sent to Spain. They had sent me photographs of her, looking splendid with her cropped ears. Now, in Switzerland, I was seeing my grandchild! In the following years, my Danes travelled far and wide and to most countries, but the thrill of that chance meeting stays a happy memory.

GERMANY

Thought of by most as the fatherland of the breed, Germany, by tradition, was the country we expected to host the Danes of splendour. There was one particular legend of a dog of which we spoke in hushed terms – the great Opal Von Harlekin. He was a brindle male of such magnificent appearance – and with show career and stud merit to match.

There was hardly a harlequin Dane of that time who did not have Eick Imperial as one of his ancestors; Diamond Von De Immenburg held a similar position in the blue colour, and Opal was the king of the fawn and brindle strains. A conservative estimate of his descendants was said to exceed 1,000. Opal became a German, Belgian, Luxembourg, Netherlands, French and Hungarian Champion. He was magnificent.

The Von Harlekin was widely admired, and we were lucky that the breeder, Herr Fuchs, was a friend of Edna Harrild of Moonsfield, and even with language barrier problems, much was learnt just listening to conversations between those two breeders.

We subscribed to the German magazine, *Deutsche Dogge*, and closely followed the breed. My friend, David Samuel brought back photographs of the Danes he had judged recently in Germany, and they still please for general make and shape – fantastic heads, size and substance, and that look of nobility.

THE SCANDINAVIAN SCENE

Many exciting dogs of most breeds are being bred in Scandinavia; Great Danes are no exception. Dane enthusiasts cannot think of Sweden without thinking of Ulla Magnusson. Ulla is considered by many to be one of the leading authorities in the world. Her Airways kennel knows no equal, and the credit for the strength of the Swedish Great Danes must go to her. Beginning in 1956 with a bitch she imported from America, in whelp, Ulla founded a dynasty.

Having recently spent time with her while judging the Swedish Great Dane Club Show, I discovered that, like me, Ulla believes in that element of luck. Ulla's came in the form of husband, Curt, who, being an airline pilot (hence the prefix) made it possible for Ulla to

Int. Ch. Hotpoints New Treasure For Batworth, at Crufts with co-owner and handler Matti Pakerinen. Imported into great Britain from Norway, this harlequin bitch took the show scene by storm.

travel the world, seeing the best Danes in every country, and wisely importing stock for her breeding programmes. Ulla has judged in Britain many times, as she has in most countries of the world. Her knowledge of the breed is so great that I will admit that when judging the breed in Finland a few years ago, I felt just a touch nervous by her presence at the ringside throughout the judging. Her approval was appreciated.

We share concern for developments in the Great Dane of today, the excessive length of back; the too pronounced forechest and the 'short on the leg' look giving us both grave misgivings. We are agreed that movement is just not good enough. We yearn for the long ground-covering stride, with forward reach and hind drive, toplines held firm, and always that look of dignity. With the benefit of Ulla's guidance, the breed is in good shape in Sweden.

In fawns, the Grand Fawns impress, as do those from the Diplomatics kennel. Competition is keen, with Danehouse and Bubackens, Muldalens and Grandline putting in strong challenges. Harlequins are most ably served by the Kingsize kennel, bred by veterinary

Ch. Hotpoints Fortuna of Walkmyll, bred in Norway by Bonnie Moen (nee Sorenson). Ably handled by Freda Lewis of Walkmyll fame. As all successful breeders and exhibitors need some element of luck, perhaps Freda's came in husband Ron, a most talented amateur photographer, who took this and many other excellent photographs.

surgeon Monica Stavenborn, whose Danes have excellent type, colour and temperament. There can be nothing but optimism for the breed in Sweden.

In Norway, the Hotpoints Danes of Borghild Moen (probably better known by her maiden name of Sorenson) dominate the show scene. Several of her Danes have been imported into Britain with great success.

I was pleased with the 100-strong entry I judged in Finland recently, greatly admiring this country's Top Dane of 1991, SFO Nuch Helsian Americano.

AUSTRALIA

Great strides have been made with the breed in Australia. Two Danes were exhibited in Australia in 1890 and were then bred with, but the breed did not really take a hold until many, many years later. Some blame the lack of interest on the anti-cropping laws; whatever the reasons, if the Australians were slower to appreciate the giant breed, they have certainly made up for lost time in recent years. Jean Lanning writing in the seventies tells us that

Ranpura Shaheed, pictured in Australia at only 22 months. Aust Ch. Ranpura Zahedi was imported to Britain, mated to a Dicarl stud dog, and this puppy was sent to Australia.

A pair of Australian Champions who eventually came to England with their breeder Marian Simpson-Wyeth. Continuing to breed with her Australian bloodlines and good English stock, Marian had the thrill of breeding the Best of Breed at Crufts in 1993. Pictured are Aust Ch. Ranpura Jahamarah Sahib and Aust Ch. Ranpura Zahedi.

"Great Danes in Australia remain rare." However, by the eighties and nineties, following judging visits to that country, the breed had developed and was in a very healthy state.

The Australian Dane breeder and exhibitor possesses great enthusiasm and stamina. The cost of importing into Australia is high, yet the enthusiasts have spent freely, bringing in stock from all parts of the world. America, Sweden, Germany and Britain have all played a part in bringing Great Danes to the fore in Australian shows. The stamina is necessary because of the vast distances covered. When I was judging a National Great Dane Specialty in Adelaide some years ago, one exhibitor bade me farewell on the Sunday evening following the after-show get-together, with the words "I must go if I want to be home by Thursday!". He had travelled 4,000 miles to show his Dane – thank goodness I had given him a first prize!

Often a cluster of shows are held together, giving exhibitors a weekend with the possibility of three or four different shows, and therefore different judges' opinions of their Danes. At the 1992 Spring Fair weekend in Sydney, my husband, Carl, judged the breed club Championship show on the Friday evening, and on Saturday morning there was a breed club Open show with S.Sinko from Slovonia judging. In the afternoon Jean Fournier from the USA officiated, and on the Sunday Spring Fair event, I had the pleasure of going over these good Great Danes.

Our placings were not always identical, but they were close, and a fawn male import from Britain took the top spot under two of the judges. This was a Drumview Dane from the Scottish Kennel of Micky Ramsey. A harlequin found favour under Carl, from the strong Warpaint kennel of David and Lesley Thorpe and Joe Diadone. This kennel has been helped by Batworth blood carrying Norwegian lines, and Asoud stock carrying German bloodlines. It was interesting to see that a baby bitch I had admired on a previous visit, Warpaint Rumour Has It, had gone on to become the GDC of NSW Great Dane of the Year in 1990, sired by Batworth Limited Edition. Another I had loved was a young fawn bitch called Merriwa Quiet Achiever – I can well understand why she made the top.

There are many good breeders in Australia producing Danes that could compete in any country in the world, including Raatu, Hildydane, Telstart, Underane, Doggenstadt, Wilksdane, Merriwa, Chezdane, Danesfield, Pridedane, Amasa, Airliebank, Leibendane, and Presentin. I really could find Danes of true breed type, correct construction, well handled, and of some quality from many sources. It was perhaps the Danelyne exhibits of Vic and Zena Place that most pleased my eye, and if I have to mention just one, then Ch. Danelyne Flash Gordon, who was Dane of his year in South Australia and of predominantly Australian breeding, which pleased me, as Australia, just like Britain, has had a surfeit of imports bringing in both good and bad features with them.

The Kochak Danes of Steve and Lois Arrowsmith have achieved great success and a string of Champions combining American, Swedish and British imports. Some British fanciers will remember Airways Adrian and Celebers Kilroy, who stayed in Britain on their way to Australia. Both quickly gained their titles in their new country, as did the Impton's, Peregrine and Kestrel, who then bred on for the kennel. Offspring included an impressive fawn bitch, Ch. Kochak Biba, and a handsome brindle male of elegant outline, Ch. Kochak Delaware, who was later to move, with his owners, Rory and Pat Lowe, to New Zealand where he was of great advantage to the breeders of that country.

I like the Danes of Australia; I like the people and their attitude to the breed and to the sport of showing dogs. It is of interest to note a tribute paid by one of the Australian Dog Magazines, *Oz Dog*, to "The Great Dane People of Australia, whose support, both as subscribers and as advertisers, along with moral support, helps assure the future of the publication." Those traits of character will, I feel sure, apply equally in the assured future of the Great Dane in Australia.

NEW ZEALAND

The breed was quite popular in the forties and fifties, with Ouborough lineage available via an import from Bill Spilstead of Australia – Ch. Warwick Royal Ruler. There was a breed club in Auckland, but by the end of the fifties interest in the breed had waned for various reasons. One factor was the hardship of the long sea voyage for dogs imported from other countries. The club folded, and the sixties were bleak years for the breed.

Between 1969 and 1971, Penny Fairclough imported three Moonsfield Danes, Tophat and Tudor Darren both having been shown with some success in England. My generation will

ABOVE: Rosemary Hubrich of New Zealand with a team of her highly successful Alquist Great Danes – plus Poodle companion!

LEFT: This handsome fawn male is NZ Ch. Alquist Virtuoso. He shows outstanding breed type with excellent strength of head and depth of muzzle. From this photograph, he looks as if he could compete successfully in any country in the world.

remember 'Hattie' (Tophat) winning a Reserve CC. She gained her NZ title, as did Ch. Telletto. Darren was injured on the boat journey which limited his show career, and he was only able to sire one litter. Anyone who breeds and shows comes to know disappointment. Imagine the heartbreak when costly importing fails to go smoothly.

The Great Dane Club was formed in the late sixties with a nucleus of about twenty Dane fanciers, and it catered for the whole of New Zealand. Nowadays its 'zone of influence' covers the northern half of the North Island. The Wellington Great Dane Club, formed in 1978, caters for the lower half of the North Island.

Probably the most consistent winners in the early seventies were the two Australian imports: the fawn bitch, Ch. Grossdane Tempest, and the fawn dog, Ch. Grossdane Steed Esquire. The first President of the GDC was Phillip Ford, who with his wife, Maud, and son, Timothy, established the successful Rathgael prefix. Early in the seventies Rosemary and Bruce Hubrich joined them in importing a blue male from the UK, Masnou Lord Samquill, and the Alquist kennel began; and it continues to this day to lead the way for the Great Danes in New Zealand.

Rosemary and Bruce began with blues and blacks. Their first fawn was Ch. Gamelin Going Places, from Ivy Wright's Gamelin kennel. Champions followed in those three colours and also brindle. The Alquist Danes have achieved Best in Show All Breeds, and Rosemary's knowledge is acknowledged by judging appointments in many other countries. The three Danes imported from the Kochak kennel (already mentioned under the Australia heading) strengthened even further the Alquist lines, and at the present time the Hubrichs are about to import frozen semen (a 'first' for Danes in NZ) which is helping to revolutionise the development of pedigree dogs 'down under'. They are to benefit from the use of semen imported from Hazel Gregory's Von Reisenhof kennels of Texas, USA.

The Gamelin kennel continued to breed Danes of merit, importing both a blue and a black from the Impton kennel, and an Underane brindle bitch from Sue Fairbairne, descended from American imports, who produced four fawn bitch Champions in one litter. A dominant stud dog in the kennel was NZ Ch. Adcote Kimber Of Sherain, sired by Lincoln Winstead Von Raeseac.

When Bob and Ive Wright retired, their property became the domain of the Mantura Danes of Craig and Benney Scott, whose strain is now further consolidated by the presence of NZ Ch. Airways On Line, a BIS All Breeds winner and a dominant stud dog. The Mainwood Danes of Brian and Gael Taylor were a force to be reckoned with, and in 1975 they imported two harlequins from Hildygarde Mooney of Sydney. The dog, Ch. Hildydane Count Amour, became the Top Winning Dane in NZ. Count was sired by the English import, Ch. Helmlake Dazzling Igor – well named, as he certainly dazzled the judges at the Pal International Show in Australia, by going BIS All Breeds at only sixteen months of age.

The Taylors also campaigned the fawn American dog, NZ Ch. Willowlakes Xmas Carrillon, who was imported into Australia by Margaret Ridgway of Adelaide. While in New Zealand Xmas Carrillon was shown nine times, won eight Best of Breeds, various Group wins, and a BIS All Breeds. His daughter, NZ Ch. Hexengold Taffeta became another top winner.

Janet and Jerry Barkas' Crestwell Danes began in Wellington, and they have maintained

NZ Ch. Alquist Look N Envy (pictured top) and NZ Ch. Alquist Da Vinchy: Two black males who have both won BIS All Breeds awards in the New Zealand show rings.

their great interest in the coloured Danes and also in the Wellington GDC, where they have been the driving force. Notable winners from their kennel include Ch. Mainwood Mystic Lady and Ch. Mainwood Misty Blue. Blessed with enthusiasm and achieving success are Brian and Marilyn Tolley of the Charlemagne prefix. Their top winner, Ch. Charlemagne Iron Maiden, was sired by the English import, The Maestro, bred and imported by Julie

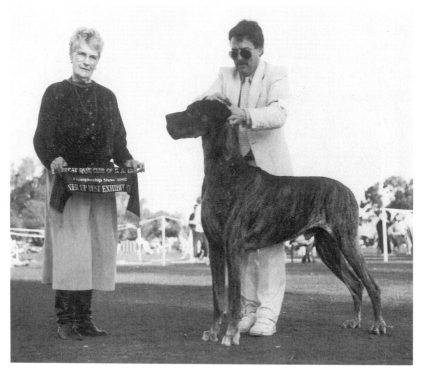

A Dane to be proud of! Aust & NZ Ch. Kochak Delaware shown at eight years of age winning BIS at South Australian Dane Specialty. Shown with handler/owner Rory Lowe and judge Hazel Gregory of the famous American Von Reisenhof Dane kennel.

Chivers. This dog's breeding goes back to Dicarl and Lincoln Winstead Von Raeseac. A new import from England of similar bloodlines should prove interesting.

The breed may not be numerically that strong in New Zealand, with an average entry of 20-30 Danes and nearing 60 as a record entry at a Club Show, but the dedication is strong and admirable and deserves every encouragement.

SOUTH AFRICA

South Africa is a country of great beauty and enormous size. In Britain, it is hard to appreciate the efforts put in by dog exhibitors in countries such as South Africa. To travel 1,000 miles to show a dog takes dedication, and the time spent at the show venue must be as pleasurable as possible. The ringside is colourful with awnings and umbrellas; ice boxes stacked high with cold drinks for dogs and humans, and barbecues on site – the food is always plentiful and of excellent quality.

Our breed has not achieved great popularity in South Africa. There are breed enthusiasts, of course, whose interest can match those of any continent. There are breed clubs serving different vast areas. The South African Great Dane Association is based in Johannesburg, while, for example, the Great Dane Club of East Africa covers Kenya – so far apart in miles – the breed lacks the opportunities available elsewhere. Great Dane entries at any show are small, and all colours are on view. In 1989 an imported harlequin from America, Ch. Thor

Court Thunder Tank Of Falkdane did make the top 100 list, all provinces, standing No.34. He is an impressive male, owned by Conrad and Anne Falkson – he even annexed a BIS at the Northern Natal KC.

The Great Dane in South Africa has always held the thread of contact with the breed worldwide, perhaps particularly in England. Older exhibitors will remember the All Round judge, Stan Kay, who had a particular affinity with our breed, judging them regularly and with obvious pleasure. Stan's son, Neil, settled in South Africa (his chosen breed was Whippets), but forging a link between the countries. Jill Coyne of the Kilcroney Danes has also given encouragement and information to the fanciers in South Africa. Several English imports gained their titles, but distances limited their effects on future breeding in the country.

South African bred Danes that have impressed include Ch. Anvin's Zanza. Mr and Mrs W.Walkfer produced consistent Champions in the seventies and eighties. By the late eighties the Macsthatch Great Danes of Pam McArthur were winning all in their path, gaining the Great Dane of the Year awards in 1987 and 1988. – combining American and English bloodlines in Ch. Macsthatch's Georgia, and supplementing their stock by importing Ch. Amberly Acres At Macsthatch from Nancy Van Der Meer of Canada, whose pedigree is a blend of Canadian and American bloodlines. Mary Scott keeps the harlequin flag flying with her Bichero Danes, Ch. Bichero Idomeneo taking BIS at the South African Great Dane Club Open in 1988. Before we leave South Africa, I would like to mention the Lea Concord Danes of Jean and Ken Leigh. I saw much to like in their Danes, particularly Ch. Lea Concord's Stetson.

Whatever country we think or write about, inevitably, some dogs and kennels most deserving of mention, will be missed. Sometimes because of a genuine memory lapse, sometimes simply lack of space. No slights are intended!

Whatever part of the world, temperament in the breed remains usually very good. It seems that breeders may change the appearance of the Great Dane, but the temperament characteristics hold true. Great Danes are most adaptable, coping with most things in life as they occur. Given luxurious surroundings they cope as to the manner born! Some of the happiest and most relaxed Danes lived with Diane and Barry Blades in Barbados. Betty Boustead sent over a couple of her lovely Wykendrift Danes who easily gained their English titles, and Ch. The High Flyer Of Dicarl frequently took BIS All Breeds in good competition. Flyer was bred by Stan Wooldrdge out of his quality Aysdaine bitch. Stan's interest was always in the care and breeding of Danes rather than exhibiting. He came to Dicarl as kennel manager, and remains to this day as part of the family. And that, perhaps, brings us back to where we began on our visit to Danes worldwide: a great family with a common bond – the breed.

Chapter Eleven

HEALTH CARE

Every owner's aim is to keep their Great Dane in good health. Provided the puppy that is purchased is strong, healthy and well bred, reared by a breeder who has given the puppy the very best of feeding, care and attention during the first couple of months of life, then, with just ordinary luck and the owner's continued tender loving care, a Great Dane should enjoy a troublefree and healthy life.

Danes are a strong and robust breed, and given a sensible diet, correct exercise, comfortable housing and some grooming, they should look and feel well. However, as we are all aware, the healthiest child or fittest adult of the human race will occasionally have health problems, which are soon overcome with correct treatment. Sensible breeders will advise new puppy purchasers to show the puppy to their veterinary surgeons within the first few days of ownership, make arrangements for inoculations, and generally build up a rapport similar to the relationship established with the family doctor. After all, the Dane is now part of the family; new owners should be encouraged to treat the new pup as they would a new baby or child in the house – with commonsense!

DIARRHOEA
This is a complex subject to cover in a paragraph or two. A puppy will often have 'loose' motions, caused by a variety of reasons – overfeeding, too much milk, something unsuitable picked up and eaten, or even stress. This should be treated by withholding food for eighteen hours or so, leaving fresh water available. When you start feeding again, offer a plainer diet, such as boiled rice or fish, or wafer biscuits with a little grated cheese. A dose or two of diarrhoea mixture (that usually given to a child in the family) can be given. If the motions are passed 'loose', very watery and more frequent, and if there is any sign of blood in them, then veterinary advice must be sought immediately.

An adult Dane suffering an upset stomach, for much the same reasons, can be treated in much the same way. If symptoms persist, then veterinary help should be sought. Never disregard diarrhoea; it could be accompanied by a rise in temperature and vomiting. These are symptoms of gastro-enteritis, a serious infection that can cause dehydration and rapid loss of condition. Prompt veterinary advice is needed; it is always better to be safe than sorry.

CUTS AND WOUNDS

Inevitably, at some time in a Dane's life, an injury of some sort will occur. Hopefully, this will only be minor. A cut, gash or wound will need cleaning with a mild disinfectant solution, and a tube of antiseptic ointment should always be to hand for treating small problems.

A larger wound may need stitching by the vet, and in order to restrict the dog's licking of the injury, it may be necessary for a protective collar, similar to an Elizabethan ruff, to be worn. The Dane may look comical or pathetic in such a device, but is is a useful aid. It is necessary to remove the collar regularly to check all is well around the dog's neck underneath, as I have seen dreadful sores occur from the constant rubbing. Occasionally, in a deep puncture, such as is caused by a dog bite, the surface may heal over leaving infection underneath. A course of antibiotics may be necessary.

Cuts to the pads are particularly difficult to deal with. Stitches are inclined to break open from pressure when the foot is put to the floor. Butterfly stitches, which are made out of strips of sticking plaster, placed criss-cross over the wound, pulling the edges together, may prove more effective. Bandage the foot well, and then use an old sock covered in a polythene bag to keep out the wet, and tape firmly in place.

STINGS

Great Danes are fascinated by insects buzzing around them, to the point of trying to catch them in their mouths. If the irritant happens to be a bee or wasp, the dog may be stung. This is not normally serious, but if the dog seems distressed, a soothing paste of bicarbonate of soda and water can be applied. I find that an antiseptic solution or lemon juice relieves a wasp sting. Should the sting be in the mouth, then apply an ice pack to reduce the inflammation, and then consult your vet.

BURNS

Should your Dane ever receive a burn or scald, speed is essential. If possible, immerse the burned area in cold water, or continually pour cold water over to ease the pain. Cover with clean tissue and if anything more than reddening of the skin occurs, then you must consult your vet.

HEAT STROKE

This is a potential danger, even if you do not live in a particularly hot climate. I recall one particularly hot summer: a couple of my twenty-week-old puppies chose to ignore the shaded areas available in their run, and they lay soaking up the sun. It did not occur to me to see any danger. However, the puppies did suffer heat stroke, with temperatures running high and on the verge of collapse. It was necessary to quickly reduce body heat. We did this by by applying ice packs – bags of frozen food will do in an emergency. The vet checked the pups over; they were really poorly, but quickly recovered.

The most common cause of heat stroke results from leaving dogs in cars. There have been so many dire warnings about the dangers of leaving dogs in cars on even a moderately warm day, that I cannot believe people continue to behave so thoughtlessly – but they do. I make no apologies for being so hard-hitting on this subject. Dogs in cars collapse and die if they are not rescued on time. Please take heed!

POISONOUS SUBSTANCES
Anyone who has ever owned a Great Dane puppy knows the characteristic habit of picking up foreign objects in the mouth. I have never had a Dane pup who did not pick up pebbles, rocks, fir-cones – anything available will do.

There is just a possibility that a puppy may pick up something poisonous. Slug pellets, weed killer, rat poison, even some common garden plants such as foxgloves, laburnum seeds, yew leaves, and some toadstools are potentially lethal. If you think your puppy has picked up something dangerous, a couple of lumps of the old-fashioned washing soda pushed down the throat will make the dog sick. This should be followed by an immediate visit to the vet. If possible, take a sample of the suspected substance with you.

TEENAGE SPOTS
The vet will probably be of little help in dealing with this Great Dane phenomenon. We have even had vets from different parts of the country, ringing, with a 'teenage spotted' Great Dane in the surgery, asking for information on the condition.

In fact, most Danes, at some time or another, get 'teenage spots' around the mouth and under the chin. They may be unsightly, but they are completely harmless. Some breeders use zinc and castor oil cream on the affected area, others use surgical spirit. However, the spots will disappear in time, so there is really nothing to worry about.

SKIN IRRITATIONS
If your Dane is persistently scratching, then something is causing the irritation. There is plenty of choice!

It could be an allergy to a new carpet or a new brand of floor cleaner; it could be the diet, possibly too rich in protein. Congested anal glands could also be to blame. Sometimes eczema will break out, characterised by the sudden appearance of large, wet, hairless patches, usually on the back or in a place accessible to the dog's teeth. With help, the cause must be found and treated.

It is likely to be fleas, lice or mange; all of which are parasites. Fleas are easily detectable by flea dirt in the dog's coat; little black specks which turn red when placed on wet paper. They can be effectively dealt with by the many excellent sprays, powders and baths on the market. It is important to treat the bedding and certain areas in the house, e.g. skirting boards, under warm radiators, as well as the dog. Lice and ear mites can be treated in a similar way.

Often owners and even experienced breeders feel great shame at having a flea problem. The only blame attached is if you allow the infestation to continue. Fleas and other parasites are easily picked up – from other dogs, from stinging nettles, hedgehogs etc. The problem is unavoidable but correctable !

Mange, whether sarcoptic mange or the much more serious demodectic mange, needs veterinary treatment.

WORMS

A Dane puppy will probably have been wormed twice or three times before leaving the breeder. The worming should continue, perhaps monthly, acting on your own veterinarian's advice, until the Dane is six months of age. From then onwards for the rest of the adult life it is a wise precaution to worm at six-monthly intervals. Tapeworms are rarely encountered in puppies, but adults can sometimes be infested. The signs are rice-like grains in the motions, often accompanied by a voracious appetite and a general loss of condition. Fleas are part of the life cycle of the tapeworm, so it is important that your Dane is kept free of all unwanted visitors.

CYSTS: SEBACEOUS AND INTERDIGITAL

Small lumps or swellings can appear from time to time. If they appear on the Dane's body, often along the back or on the neck, they are probably sebaceous cysts. These are non-malignant, so do not worry. They are caused by congestion of sebum (a waxy substance) in the glands of the skin. Sometimes they will erupt and may need attention from your vet. A course of antibiotics or even minor surgery may be needed.

When these swellings appear between the dog's toes, they are called interdigital cysts. They can be painful and cause lameness, but they are curable. Ask your vet for advice – bathing with warm salt water may help.

THE WAGGING TAIL

This is a problem you may encounter, just because your Dane is healthy and happy. A Great Dane can wag the tail with such gusto – you will know just how much it hurts if a wagging tail makes contact with your legs. If the surface hit by the wagging tail lacks the soft cushioning effect of your body, and comes into contact with wood or concrete walls, an injury results.

It is a real problem, once begun, as it is impossible to stop a healthy, happy Dane wagging the tail. A few specks of blood and the tiniest wound rapidly become serious with continued wagging. It is therefore necessary to protect the wounded tail tip. Treat as you would any wound, cleansing and applying antibiotic ointment: bandage and apply some protection to the area – the inside of a toilet roll or suitably sized plastic tubing, is ideal. Bind this on to the tail end, hoping the protective tubing will act as cushioning between tail and hard surfaces. This bandaging will need changing, recleaning and redressing daily.

The other problem is persuading the Dane to leave the bandage alone. The Elizabethan collar may need to be used to stop the Dane dismantling the protective covering. Some tails heal swiftly and well, and the problem does not recur. Sometimes, amputation of part of the tail is the only answer. If you should ever have to resort to that drastic solution, then do not just have a few inches removed, for the problem will keep recurring. Ask your veterinary surgeon to leave only about nine inches of tail; long enough for the Dane to wag, but not long enough to damage.

After months of pain and effort, one of my bitches, Lise, was finally left with nine inches of tail. She loved it! She was so proud of her 'different' tail. Owners of the breed will know that a typical Dane habit is to 'find and bring a present': this could be one of your best cushions, or outside, a Dane will busy around looking for anything, a stone, a stick, just anything to present to a friend. Lise was awfully good at this game, bringing some quite unsuitable things over the years. However, this all changed with the new style short tail. That became the present! Her back end would be presented, with the short appendage wagging away for admiration from her loved ones! Hopefully, tail damage will never happen to your Dane. Most Danes go through their lives without encountering the problem. If it does happen, do not despair; it is not the end of the world.

BLOAT/DISTENTION/TORSION

Most of the giant and deep-chested breeds are susceptible to this terrifying condition. It is caused by fermenting foods releasing gas into the stomach, which, in the most severe cases, causes the stomach to twist. This is a most serious condition and speed is of the essence in seeking veterinary attention.

Owners should be warned that a perfectly fit and healthy Dane can suddenly 'bloat'. The main symptom is a rapid swelling of the stomach, making it hard and distended, and causing the dog great pain. Attempts to vomit will bring up a foamy, sticky substance, and attempts to defecate, with much discomfort, may be observed. I cannot stress too strongly the seriousness of a suspected bloat condition. *It really is a life or death situation requiring immediate veterinary treatment.* You must rush your Dane to the vet's surgery, where an emergency operation may save your Dane's life.

This is all we can say with certainty about this dreaded problem. Theories abound. For as long as I can remember, the problem has been discussed, information collected, and reasons sought. As yet there is no answer, but research continues.

I have known Danes suffer a single case of bloat, survive the operation and the post-operative shock which is often the killer, and then live long and bloat-free lives afterwards. Some believe that, once stricken, a Dane is more susceptible to the condition, and in fact there are Danes who have survived two or three attacks of bloat. In our kennels we only ever had three cases; only one survived and did not have a recurrence of the condition.

Sensible suggested precautions include feeding the Dane twice a day, involving two smaller meals rather than one large one. Fresh drinking water should be available at all times, and exercise should be restricted for a couple of hours after feeding.

COMMONSENSE OWNERSHIP

I have often wondered where the term 'commonsense' came from, as, in fact, the virtue is anything but 'common'. The aim is to achieve a balance between the 'panicking and over-reacting' syndrome, and the 'leave it, it might go away' syndrome. It is claimed that most of us, reading a medical dictionary, would experience feelings of hypochondria, imagining we had symptoms of some ailment or another. Please do not read this chapter and begin to worry.

Your Great Dane may well go through life enjoying the rudest of good health. But should your Dane appear unwell, then seek veterinary advice too soon rather than too late. Many problems may be nipped in the bud, whereas if left to become acute, the condition may become difficult and expensive to cure. Good vets will understand the owner who seeks a consultation for something that is is only minor, but they will not be so understanding if an animal is caused unnecessary discomfort because of an owner's reluctance to seek professional help. Use your commonsense; feed, house and exercise your Dane with care, and share with your friend a full, happy and healthy life.

THE VETERAN DANE

Great Danes are wonderful in old age. They become more loyal, lovable and characterful with each passing year. An elderly Dane can combine unspeakable naughtiness with such grey, masked dignity – providing memories you will treasure long after they have gone.

I remember Tarbaby, the most elegant and ladylike Dane, arising from the settee, aged nine-and-a-half, to stroll across to where we were giving afternoon tea to some rather smart visitors, and proceed to lap, noisily and messily, the contents of the milk jug on the tea tray. We were all too stunned to stop her. She had *never* done such a thing before! She then emitted a loud noise, expressing satisfaction and proving that her digestive system was in good order, and sashayed back to the settee, settled herself with aristocratic grace and then looked me straight in the eye – daring comment!

There was Domonic, who as a youngster had received a minor bite on a front foot after irritating an older Dane, and he never let us forget it. In his dotage he would get away with any misdemeanour by whimpering and lifting for inspection that once-injured foot, with a reproachful expression that clearly accused us of negligence in his youth, exonerating him from any blame in his old age!

I would go so far as to say the only drawback to loving a Great Dane is that they are not long-lived. I have had Danes live to ten and eleven years; I have known Danes live to fourteen years – but many go earlier than that and however long they live, it is not long enough. At six or seven years old, some Danes feel and show their years and when the time comes that they cannot live a happy and pain-free life, it is time to say goodbye. You will have given them warmth and comfort through the years, and you must allow them their dignity at the end.

A Dane is embarrassed by incontinence, distressed by immobility, and saddened when quality of life has gone. At such a time, your Dane may go to sleep and not awaken. If help is needed, you must give it. Do not subject your Dane to a vet's waiting room; ask the vet to come to your home, and you will be able to hold your Dane in your arms at the very end. You may be able to provide a final resting-place in your garden, or there are now pet crematoriums or burial grounds.

Do not try to contain or hide your grief. Tears do help, and Dane-owning friends will give you much support and understanding. At the loss of each and every Dane, I would immediately ring my friend, Audrey Sheppard, who would cry with me, sharing and knowing my feelings and helping because of that. I am crying now, writing this, and I know Audrey will when she reads it!

This is the depth of love a Great Dane inspires. For that reason, allow your thoughts to go to a new puppy. Many people endure weeks and months of sadness and a house seemingly empty, as they cannot bear the thought of replacing an old friend or of a similar sadness a number of years hence. Understandable perhaps, misguided almost certainly, as eventually they will succumb, and how that new puppy will help to fill the void – easing the pain, not only with the affection the new puppy brings, but also with a Great Dane pup to look after, very little free time is left for sadness.

Something Muriel Osborne said to me in my early years comes back and comforts me often. I was grieving the loss of a very favourite dog, and Muriel understood and told me that, one day, that dog would return. Sometime in the future I would recognise that old friend in a current Dane: perhaps not just in physical appearance, but in temperament and characteristics, in his comprehension of situations and feelings; in a special familiar bond between us; I would just *know* it was him and that he had returned.

I mentioned this story on one occasion in my Breed Notes in the weekly dog papers. I had more response from all the world than I ever had on any other subject – and this was not just from Great Dane owners. It seems many people have 'felt' the return of a favourite. It has certainly happened to me. By the time Smooth Sailing was six or seven months old, I knew she was my lovely Rosie, although her pet name was Mavis, and, of course, she responded to that name. I only had to say "Rosie", in any tone of voice and any situation, and she would come and be with me, bringing Rosie's traits and personality with her.

A new puppy will not replace your old friend. A new puppy will bring new love and enjoyment all their own, and sometime, perhaps sometime, a new puppy will bring twice the amount of love and happy memories.

Chapter Twelve

INHERITED DISEASES

AN ILLUSTRATED GUIDE FOR BREEDERS AND OWNERS BY MAGGIE DOWN, BRUCE MACDONALD, AND JOY SINCLAIR, October 1991.

KEY TO CATEGORIES
**** Serious major genetic defects
*** Common genetic defects
** Less common or serious
* Genetic but uncommon

CERVICAL VERTEBRAE INSTABILITY/CERVICAL SPONDYLOPATHY (CVI) 'WOBBLER SYNDROME' ****
DESCRIPTION: A degenerative condition which affects Great Danes. The basic problem occurs due to compression of the spinal cord, when the cervical vertebrae (neck bones) are malformed, extruding or protruding. In extreme cases, the rear end of the dog does not seem able to support its weight. The cervical vertebrae are, during the rapid growth stage, i.e. 2-4 months, very vulnerable to damaging changes. Age of noticeable onset in Great Danes is approximately 3 to 5 months. The condition is non-painful.
SIGNS: The first sign for an unsuspecting owner is ataxia (i.e. unco-ordinated or drunken-like movement) most commonly in the hindquarters. The hind legs may take on a wide gait when standing. There may be difficulty in turning and the hind legs may cross over. Often there is difficulty in getting into position for urinating and defaecating.
CAUSE/AETIOLOGY: a) Inherited.
b) Over-feeding, over-supplementation, incorrect diet can be contributory factors.
INVESTIGATIONS (VET): a) Reflex tests.
b) X-ray (not always conclusive).
c) Myleogram (Vet College).
TREATMENT: a) Medication (e.g. prednisolone) – but only in mild cases.
b) Surgery – fixation of the vertebrae involved (but will, if successful, only stabilise the condition). Although medication is usually as successful as surgery, neither will return the dog to normal.
PROGNOSIS: Extremely poor. This unfortunate condition can only be prevented by a combination of:-
a) Not breeding from affected stock.

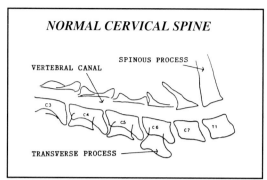

CERVICAL VERTEBRAL INSTABILITY (CVI)
"WOBBLER SYNDROME" now known as CERVICAL SPONDYLOPATHY

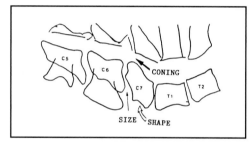

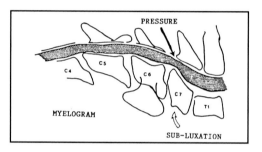

b) Careful attention to diet during growth.
c) Ensuring steady growth of puppies up to the age of 6 months.

OSTEOCHONDRITIS DISSECANS (OCD) ***
DESCRIPTION: A condition which usually affects the shoulder joints, but can affect the stifle and hock joints. It is commonly bilateral. In Osteochondritis Dissecans there is disturbance of the maturing cartilage of the affected joint. The head of the bone and the affected cartilage are deprived of essential nutrients and the cartilage becomes thickened and the bone fails to mature properly, causing flattening. Age of onset 4-9 months. Males are affected more than females.
CAUSE: Inherited. Accelerated by mineral over-supplementation and over-nutrition. Trauma – e.g. over-exercising of puppies.
SIGNS: Intermittent or persistent limping from the affected limb; stiffness on rising.
INVESTIGATIONS (VET): X-ray.
TREATMENT: a) Rest (complete). b) Surgery.
PROGNOSIS: Outlook excellent: following surgery, within 6-8 weeks the dog should make a full recovery. It is recommended that even though treated successfully, dogs once affected with OCD should not be part of a breeding programme.

HIP DYSPLASIA ***
DESCRIPTION: It is a condition affecting one or both hip joints. The hip joint is a ball-and-socket joint that is capable of a wide range of movement. The hips can be affected both in the socket (acetabulum) and/or at the head of the femur. In an affected dog the growth of the muscle takes

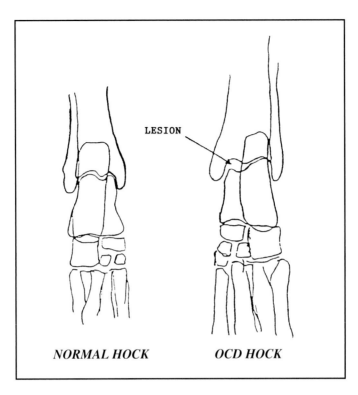

LESION

NORMAL HOCK   *OCD HOCK*

longer than that of the bone, thereby causing a pulling apart of the ball from the socket. Hip dysplasia can cause mild to severe symptoms culminating in a dislocated joint.

CAUSES: Inherited; rapid weight gain in puppies; over-exercising puppies and rough play; trauma.

SIGNS: Pain (but not always); limping (mild to severe); stiffness (particularly on rising).

INVESTIGATIONS (VET): X-ray of the hip joints.

TREATMENT: Conservative: Limit exercise; avoid weight gain; keep in warm, dry environment; anti-arthritic or pain-killing drugs (analgesics) may provide some relief, temporarily.

Surgical: A variety of techniques are available including:

a) Sectioning the pectineus muscle.

b) Sectioning the pectineus and adductor magnus muscles.

c) Pectinal myotomy or tenonectomy.

d) Repositioning the acetabulum by pelvic osteotomy (in young animals where no joint disease is present).

All the above techniques require above-average surgical skill and although they may decrease the progression of the problem, they will not prevent all subluxation, nor will they prevent degenerative joint disease. The most attractive treatment for advanced hip dysplasia is total hip replacement and although this procedure is becoming most practical from a technical aspect, the almost prohibitive cost of surgery limits its use. Clinically affected stock should not be bred from.

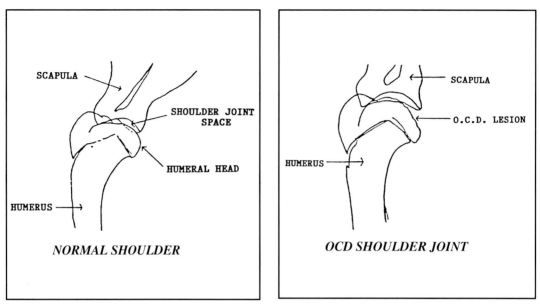

NORMAL SHOULDER

OCD SHOULDER JOINT

UNUNITED ANCONEAL PROCESS **

DESCRIPTION: The anconeal process is a part of the ulna bone (of the fore limb). Ununited anconeal process is a fusion defect of the elbow joint which results in constant movement of the joint, thereby causing it to be unstable. The condition can be unilateral or bilateral. Age of onset 5-7 months.

CAUSE: Inherited; metabolic abnormalities e.g. hormone imbalance.

SIGNS: Pain; lameness; fluid-type swelling on the side of the elbow joint; limited movement of elbow joint.

INVESTIGATIONS (VET); X-ray.

TREATMENT: Surgical removal of the anconeal process.

PROGNOSIS: Good, but lameness may persist and arthritis will sooner or later occur. Treated dogs should not be part of a breeding programme.

CARDIOMYOPATHIES ****

DESCRIPTION: Heart muscle disease which occurs in the absence of any known disease or any abnormality of function. This definition can be used to describe a number of conditions which come under the umbrella of cardiomyopathies. Usually there is enlargement of the heart and fibrosis of the heart muscle. In Danes the heart dilates and there is a lower volume of blood pumped out per heart beat.

CAUSE: Inherited.

SIGNS: Those of heart failure; lack of exercise tolerance; shortness of breath; bluish tinge to gums and eyes (by this stage the disease is well advanced); fainting; heart murmurs: (diagnosed by vet).

TREATMENT: Treat as symptoms occur – e.g. a diuretic drug (eliminates excess fluid from the body).

PROGNOSIS: Poor. Survival time is between 6-12 months after onset of treatment. Affected stock should not be bred from.

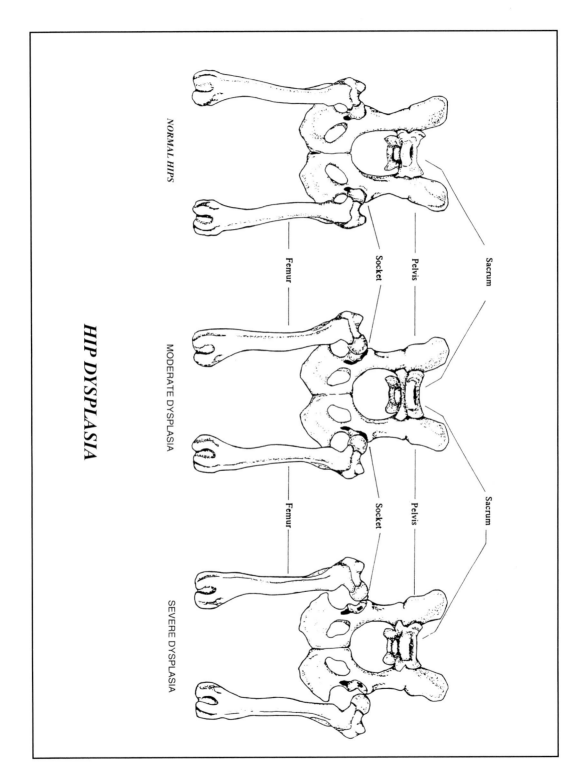

HIP DYSPLASIA

NORMAL HIPS

MODERATE DYSPLASIA

SEVERE DYSPLASIA

Femur

Socket

Pelvis

Sacrum

Femur

Socket

Pelvis

Sacrum

CALCINOSIS CIRCUMSCRIPTA **

DESCRIPTION: This is a condition where deposits of calcium form on soft tissue of the body. It is non-painful. It occurs usually in young dogs of the large breeds. The blood calcium level generally stays within normal limits.

CAUSES: Inherited; congenital.

SIGNS: The presence of one or more swellings which are hard. Symptoms vary depending on where in the body the swellings occur – e.g. ataxia may result from spinal compression if the calcium deposits are on the spinal column (this is not a common site, fortunately).

INVESTIGATIONS (VET): X-ray.

TREATMENT: Surgical removal of calcified tissue.

PROGNOSIS: Excellent following surgical removal of the swellings.

DEAFNESS *

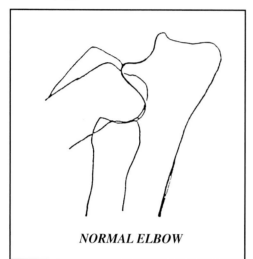

NORMAL ELBOW

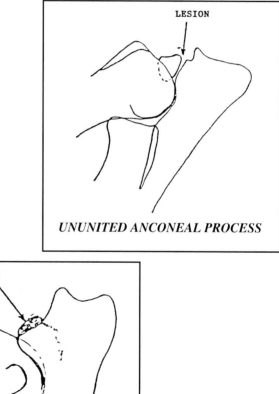

UNUNITED ANCONEAL PROCESS

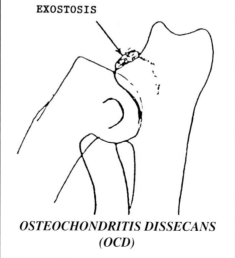

OSTEOCHONDRITIS DISSECANS
(OCD)

DESCRIPTION: There is atrophy (wasting) of the specialised nerve endings and membrana labyrinth. The most likely cause of deafness in the Dane results from abnormalities within the cochlea (in the inner ear) where damage to the delicate hairs and surrounding membranes quickly creates irreversible collapse of the part of the ear (sensory deafness). The merle gene (in harlequins) is frequently responsible for congenital deafness. Middle and outer ear abnormalities may also cause deafness (conductive deafness), but this is rare and can be treated.

CAUSES: Inherited – as described above; unknown causes; viral and other infections (i.e. acquired deafness); congenital.

SIGNS: No/little response to commands; difficult to wake; aggressive/defensive behaviour; becomes distressed when separated from companion.

Owner may not notice until dog is 12 months or older.

INVESTIGATIONS (VET): Auditory function tests; reflex tests.

TREATMENT: Usually none, unless deafness is of the conductive type.

PROGNOSIS: Poor – but need not limit an active life if owner exercises extreme care and attention.

DISTORTION OF MEMBRANA NICTITANS **

DESCRIPTION: The membrana nictitans is the dog's third and most important eyelid. Part of its function is to protect the cornea by producing a film-like substance. The distorted eye lid curls forward in this condition.

CAUSE: Inherited.

SIGNS: Pain; dog rubbing affected eye; discharge; conjunctivitis; the owner may actually see a kink on the eyelid.

TREATMENT: Surgical – Excision of the everted cartilage.

PROGNOSIS: Good following surgery – complications can be long term:-

a) chronic conjunctivitis (depending upon the degree of surgery necessary).

b) secondary entropion.

c) ulceration of the cornea.

STOCKARD'S DISEASE *

DESCRIPTION: This condition is a form of progressive paralysis of a flaccid (floppy) nature. The paralysis can be slight (incomplete) or total. The underlying feature is early degeneration of the cells involved. It affects young Danes.

VON WILLEBRAND'S DISEASE *

DESCRIPTION: This wonderfully named disease occurs when Von Willebrand's factor is deficient in the blood. The factor is involved in the clotting process (haemostasis).

CAUSE: Inherited.

SIGNS: Excessive or prolonged bleeding following trauma or surgery; epistaxis (nose bleed); bleeding from the gums.

INVESTIGATIONS: Test for bleeding time, and for levels of the relevant factors.

TREATMENT: Following a bleeding episode – plasma or fresh blood is administered.

MEGAOESOPHAGUS **

DESCRIPTION: This is enlargement of the oesophagus. The mechanisms involved in passing food to the stomach (peristalsis and sphincter control) do not function properly and food is retained in the oesophagus. Often food passes down the trachea (windpipe) and causes pneumonia. Appetite is usually normal.

CAUSE: Inherited; in older dogs it can be acquired.

SIGNS: Thin, weak, depressed dog; soft, dry cough; regurgitation (not vomiting) of undigested food and fluids; upper respiratory tract infections sometimes occur with accompanied discharge from the nose.

INVESTIGATIONS (VET): X-ray and/or Barium swallow.

TREATMENT: Medical; surgical; neither with much success. Feed affected dogs from a high platform, with the dog standing on his/her hind legs (vertical).

PROGNOSIS: Poor. Death from pneumonia caused from infection of inhaled foodstuffs is common. Weight loss generally continues because food cannot be utilised properly by the body. Affected stock should not be bred from.

ENTROPION ***

DESCRIPTION: Inward turning eyelids affecting one or both eyes, resulting in the eyelashes scratching the surface of the eyeball; this generally results in corneal ulceration and possible perforation of the cornea.

CAUSE: Inherited; acquired non-spastic; acquired spastic.

SIGNS: Irritation; running eyes and general discomfort.

TREATMENT: Surgical correction, but not before 6 months of age due to the changing structure of the eye and skull prior to this period.

PROGNOSIS: Following surgery, prognosis is excellent. If left untreated serious ulceration will develop, leading to total blindness. Affected stock should not be bred from.

ECTROPION **

DESCRIPTION: A condition where the lower eyelid turns outwards, resulting in exposure of the conjunctiva and cornea. Often causes the dog owner concern because of the objectionable appearance rather than through its relationship to any disease.

CAUSE: Inherited; injury to part or all of facial nerves. Eyelid injury and poor surgery may result in cicatrix (fibrous tissue after the healing of a wound).

SIGNS: Discharge from the eyes; facial nerve function; chronic conjunctivitis; keratitis; infection and an unsightly appearance.

TREATMENT: Extremely thorough examination prior to surgery due to the many complex situations that may be present, e.g. facial paralysis, when a careful neurologic examination is necessary.

PROGNOSIS: Following surgery is usually very good. Affected stock should not be bred from, and may not be shown in the USA.

Thanks to Jason Barley BVetMed PhD MRCVS and Claire Gardner BVMS MRCVS for their much appreciated help with technical detail.